The Spice Merchant's Daughter

The Spice Merchant's Daughter

RECIPES AND
SIMPLE SPICE BLENDS FOR THE
AMERICAN KITCHEN

CHRISTINA AROKIASAMY

CLARKSON POTTER
NEW YORK

*Right: pure chile powder and fresh curry leaves;
frontispiece, clockwise from top: Ginger-Garlic Paste (page 59),
Roasted Chile Paste (page 61), Perfect Peanut Sauce (page 66),
and Seafood Spice Paste (page 62)*

Published in the United States by Clarkson Potter/Publishers,
an imprint of the Crown Publishing Group, a division of
Random House, Inc., New York.
www.crownpublishing.com
www.clarksonpotter.com

CLARKSON POTTER is a trademark and POTTER with colophon
is a registered trademark of Random House, Inc.

Library of Congress Cataloging-in-Publication Data

Arokiasamy, Christina.
The Spice merchant's daughter: recipes and simple spice blends for the
American kitchen / Christina Arokiasamy.—1st ed.
          p.   cm.
1. Cookery (Spices)   2. Cookery, Southeast Asian.   I. Title.
TX819.A1A77 2008
    641.6'383—dc22   2007050015

ISBN 978-0-307-39628-0

Printed in the United States of America

*Design by Marysarah Quinn
Map by Max Werner*

10 9 8 7 6 5 4 3 2 1

FIRST EDITION

To the memory of my mother,
Rosalind Dorairaj,
my constant strength, the beacon that lights up
my path in my journey of life,
always in my heart to keep my passion for cooking alive.

To my "second mother,"
Philomena Benedict,
who through her warm and giving nature
cared for me like her own daughter.

And to my readers,
that you may come to love spices
through the stories I tell and
the recipes I have penned.

Contents

Introduction

It was the aroma. The exotic scent of spices: rich, alluring, and almost magical. A scent that would sometimes overpower the freshness in the air and sometimes subtly mingle with it to create a tantalizing bouquet. A scent that would always bring me back to my childhood. My life has been symbiotic with that of spices. Growing up as a spice merchant's daughter in a rustic, British colonial house in Malaysia may seem like a world away, but to this day memories of my childhood come flooding in with even the slightest whiff of spice.

Jade-green lime and tamarind trees lined the cobbled driveway leading to our main house; the sweet-smelling tamarind pods hung like garlands from the trees, welcoming the constant throngs of visitors who must have felt as if they were entering my mother's secret spice domain. As I close my eyes, I hear my mother's warm voice invariably calling out "If only I had extra hands to help me finish my task before the rain comes" while she washed and dried spices in the large weathered courtyard. An old mortar and a heavy grinding stone—both heirlooms from my great-grandmother—stood in the corner, bearing testimony to the toil my mother went through daily to support us.

Spices have always been close to the heart of my family. My great-great-grandfather on my mother's side, Charles Anthony, was captain of a merchant ship owned by the English East India Company in the early nineteenth century. He traveled the trade routes transporting priceless spices and other goods to and from India, Malaya, and the islands of the Indonesian archipelago. My great-grandfather's family lived in the Portuguese colony of Trancobar, a coastal town in the district of Tamil Nadu, since 1666. Historically, Trancobar was a major Portuguese spice center with trade links to Malacca and the Indonesian islands.

My maternal grandfather was born in 1882 and settled in Rangoon, Burma, in the late nineteenth century and later ran a printing press. He and my grand-

mother, Marie Theresa Anthony, had six children, my mother, Rosalind, being the fourth. Life in Rangoon was typically centered around building a family until 1937, when Burma separated from India. Riots broke out in Rangoon in 1938, caused by Indian-Burmese antagonism, fueled by Indian landlords and moneylenders. Indians in Burma were hit with a severe depression that forced many Indian merchants to return to India. Instead, my grandparents, my mother, then eleven years old, and her siblings took part in the grim migration to Malaya (known as Malaysia following its independence from the British in 1957). Those were, perhaps, their darkest and most frightening days, when the family uprooted and relocated to a new country they knew little of, with only the belongings on their backs.

My grandparents settled in Malacca, a bustling center where the spice trade ruled nearly everyone's daily life. And that's when they started trading spices. My mother later followed suit, opening a small spice business of her own in Kuala Lumpur, where she had moved when she married. My father worked at the department of health and while he couldn't help my mother with the day-to-day running of her business, he was extremely supportive in his own way, such as by taking care of the cooking on Sundays. It was through her constant buying, washing, and drying of spices that I first became enchanted with them.

As a schoolgirl, I could always smell my house before I could see it. When my turmeric-colored school bus pulled in front of our gate, I would run home impatiently. The rich aroma of beef curry tenderly prepared with fresh, home-ground spices seemed to carry my tiny legs. My mother was much like a scientist, experimenting with a variety of spices to flavor food. Once the lunch was set on the table, the engagement was nothing short of a feast to be relished with gusto, and even before lunch was over I would begin wondering what was planned for dinner. Cooking, like the spice business, was a daily way of life for me and my family.

On weekly spice-drying days, the veranda turned into a bright canvas painted with spices, all arranged on zinc plates for drying under the heat of the tropical sun. And from the brilliant reds, yellows, greens, and a dozen other shades in every imaginable shape, size, and texture, an irresistible aroma of cumin seeds, coriander seeds, mustard seeds, nutmeg, peppercorns, cardamom, ginger, and chiles wafted throughout the yard and house, enveloping me in their perfume. I loved to let the tiny round coriander seeds run through my fingers. Was this what snow felt like? I would pick up cardamom buds and gently savor their scent, relishing the thought of my mother's buttery cardamom rice pilaf and fennel-roasted chicken.

r anise

cumin seeds

curry powder

cinnamon sticks

Lemon Pepper Rub
(page 51)

ground turmeric

n pods

nutmeg

coriander seeds

Green Seafood Rub
(page 52)

Once the spices were dry, I would help my mother fill brown gunnysacks with them. My small hands stained with turmeric, I daydreamed about my favorite dessert: kaseri, a soft turmeric-colored semolina tea cake with plump raisins and sweet cashews hidden inside. (My hands were always stained yellow. "Look at that girl with yellow hands," the girls at school would tease.) We fastened the spice-filled sacks with strips of bamboo to protect the spices on the short truck ride to the Ishweri mill, a rickety, unimpressive facility tucked away between slanting coconut trees. I hardly noticed the mill at Jalan Tenggiri, in Bangsar, until it made a coughing noise, expelling a cloud of spice dust as the machines chugged away in the distance.

I sat on a small wooden stool in the corner of the mill, desperately attempting to cover my mouth and nose with a little handkerchief, my eyes fixed on my mother, a true culinary expert. I'll never know how my mother had the energy to go through the weekly routine of preparing the spices and transporting them to the mill for grinding. Like an army sergeant on the square, she would yell out precise instructions like "Ensure that the chiles are ground into fine powder" to machine operators, men often completely colored by the dust, wearing masks to keep it out of their nostrils. Heeding her wishes, the workers busily poured spices into hoppers, large funnel-shaped containers that would feed the spices into the mill.

After the spices were ground, they were spread out to cool in a shallow wooden bed before being packed into plastic bags to prevent moisture and mold from setting in. Struggling to keep my eyes open in the spice-dust-filled air, I would watch the mill workers place our spice-filled bags in cardboard boxes and seal them, each box manifesting the reward of my mother's toil and love for the trade.

These were the spices we sold at the bustling Central Market in Kuala Lumpur. Along the market's narrow path, old men in their traditional sarongs or dhotis would be sitting idly, chewing on betel leaves and watching the world go by, while women in colorful saris would walk the market street bargaining for spices. The lemongrass scent from incense sticks, the rumble of local tunes, and the rich tapestry of the merchandise mixed with the vibrant crowd to create a kaleidoscope of colors at this unique place.

But above all, the Central Market exuded an aroma of mixed spices from hundreds of little shops. The chatter of merchants would grow louder as their facial expressions and hands punctuated their sales pitches. The more enterprising ones offered "panas panas" ("hot hot") curry puffs as they placed sample packets of masala in the hands of the buyers. Bare hands neatly heaped the mini-mountains of fiery ground masalas in gunnysacks, a vivid color palette: golden yellow turmeric powder, burning red chile powder, and earthy brown cumin, coriander, and cinnamon powders. Ready-mixed spice rubs, like balls of colored dough, were spooned onto freshly cut and cleaned square banana leaves that, once sealed, locked in the masala's moisture. Whole spices like cinnamon sticks, nutmeg, anise, caraway, cloves, and cardamom whispered their magic to the throngs of customers who visited the market daily.

During my childhood, everything and anything to do with spices could be found in the Central Market. It seemed to me that this was the kingdom of spices. Little did I know then that spices had once arrived from as far away as Spain and Portugal on ships laden with the humble chile pepper. The Indian and Arab traders introduced ground coriander, cumin, pepper, and ginger. At this crossroads of the spice trade, Southeast Asian cooks developed a mastery for flavoring, combining the spices introduced by foreign traders and skillfully blending these with indigenous spices from the region. (Although in most countries you can find spices sold in supermarkets, Southeast Asian cooks still prefer to buy spices from merchants' stalls.)

Our spice stall at the Central Market always had ornamental garlands made from fresh jasmine flowers, with wreaths of garlic dangling over bins of lentils, fresh tamarind packets, and chutney and pickle bottles—and, of course, neatly arranged bins with mounds of cumin, cardamom, pepper, and coriander in an endless parade of spices. Almost all the masala mixes for marinades, the dried herbs, and the roasted spices were home blended using my family's generation-old secret formulas and had in them my mother's passion and soul as added flavor. Our Central Market stall would brim with home cooks and seasoned curry connoisseurs purchasing fiery masalas for chicken curry. The Malay cooks would prefer a wet masala like green curry paste. Chinese cooks would favor fish masala, and the Indians would load their baskets with ginger-garlic paste, lemon pepper, and tandoori spice.

Across from the spice bazaar were rows of local butchers and restaurants. At the beginning of the trading day, their owners were the first to arrive, offering select lamb portions in exchange for fresh spices. The bartered spices would end up in food served at the restaurants. Tender chicken sautéed with onion and garlic accented with chiles, mackerel gently moistened with tomato sambal, crabs stir-fried with pepper masala, delicious vegetable biryani—all these drew scores of hungry patrons, who had sometimes traveled long distances to savor this lush cuisine. The secret was in the special merchant's masalas.

My mother, nicknamed "Doctor Masala," never shied away from an opportunity to preach the benefits of purchasing fresh spices at the market, deftly dishing out her tips for the best rice pilaf or beef curry. She was quick, too, to give out recipes for health. Saffron adds warmth to life, cinnamon prevents colds, and ginger relieves swelling—ideal for pregnant women.

Although spices were in my blood, and I enjoyed helping my mother at the market, I ended up pursuing a degree in public relations. When asked to mount a public relations campaign for the Hyatt Hotel in Kuala Lumpur, I inevitably found myself in the hotel's kitchen, exchanging recipes with the chef. From public relations, I moved on to own a motivational training consultancy. My clients became my friends through the sharing of food recipes, and during lunch breaks I would spend time browsing through my collection of cookbooks and food magazines, feeding my growing interest in upgrading my culinary skills to the professional level.

I joined the Hyatt Regency in Malaysia to start my journey of cooking in professional kitchens. To embrace the cooking traditions of the neighboring Southeast Asian countries, I continued my culinary training at Jimbaran Bali's Four Seasons Resort, Thailand's Four Seasons Resort in Chiang Mai, and later worked directly with the owner of Wandee Culinary Institute in Thailand.

In 1994 I migrated to the United States, settling in Oahu, Hawaii. In my new home, I made simple home-cooked meals like fried rice and sambals. The fragrance from my kitchen would waft across to the homes of my new neighbors, prompting them to remark, "I've never smelled anything as aromatic as this before." And so I invited them over for dinner. They enjoyed my cooking, leading some to ask, "Could you please show me how to cook this dish?" This was how my newfound

Clockwise from top left: Cardamom Butter Rice with Sultanas (page 181), Green Apple and Nutmeg Chutney (page 196), Green Beans and Carrots with Cumin Seeds (page 107), and Whole Roasted Chicken in Tamarind Butter Sauce (page 122),

friendships with the people around me blossomed, leading me to start my own informal cooking classes.

After I married and had my first son, Anton, we moved to Seattle, Washington, where I started teaching culinary classes on Southeast Asian cuisine at colleges and gourmet schools. My students' interest in healthy cooking for their families, combined with my culinary knowledge and my mother's coaching, gave me the enthusiasm to open The Spice Merchant's Cooking School.

In my years of teaching, I have learned that people choose to attend my culinary classes because they want to replicate the tantalizing flavors of Southeast Asian cuisine they have tasted in restaurants. However, they somehow have the preconceived notion that its preparation is difficult and time consuming. On the contrary, adding Southeast Asian flair to weeknight meals can be easy and delicious. The key is to prepare fresh spice pastes and dried spice rubs in advance and then store them in the freezer and cupboard. With these flavor-packed mixes in your cooking arsenal, there is no fuss of chopping and grinding spices for each meal. I learned this useful approach from my mother, who by doing so had enough time not only to run her spice business but also to care for my brother and me and prepare healthy meals at home daily.

The recipes in the chapters that follow teach you how to use spices, herbs, and seasoning sauces to enhance the depth and flavor of everyday meals. Eventually, once you learn to taste ingredients, you can decide how much of a particular seasoning to add without measuring. I always encourage my students to cook with their senses to bring a dish together. This means eyeballing the browning of onions, hearing the popping of mustard seeds, and smelling the aromatic sizzle of curry leaves as they release their scent in the air. Recipes are mainly guides to build on. Mastering a few simple spice blends frees you to create recipes to suit your own palate.

Frequently, many of my students consider ingredients such as lemongrass, chiles, sweet basil, kaffir limes, galangal, and fish sauce "Thai ingredients." I don't really blame them, as these have become synonymous with the continuous mislabeling of ingredients on restaurant menus and in many grocery shops throughout North America. These ingredients may be in Thai food, but they belong more broadly to Southeast Asian culinary traditions. The herbs, spices, and aromatic condiments widely grown throughout this region are used differently in different cultures, giving food a subtle variety of flavors.

In Malaysia, food cooked with spices is introduced to children at an early age. School canteens dish out stir-fried noodles with fresh aromatics, mild chicken curries, fried chicken with masalas, coconut rice with shrimp sambal, and a lot more. Having food laced with spices is part and parcel of our culture, and our palate gets accustomed to this. When I cook for my children here in America, I expose them to spices slowly, starting with aromatic spices a little at a time in food. Gradually they enjoy the flavor of spiced food, provided it is not "spicy," and does not contain cayenne or chiles. In my kitchen, I keep saltshakers filled with my children's favorite seasonings. One contains ground mild spices, a blend of paprika, cinnamon, garlic salt, a little sugar, and fennel; another, labeled "kids' herb rub," is made from peppercorns, oregano, thyme, sage, and garlic salt, which my children help put together. I use these to coat chicken or fish before cooking, and they love it. It is heartening to know that my children are absorbing the heart and soul of my mother's legacy as they grow up. By introducing them to seasonings and sauces, I am getting them accustomed to a mix of Western and Eastern flavors, but more important, fostering in them an appreciation of flavorful, healthy food.

My mother's lessons on life, spices, and new beginnings will always run in my blood. As spices were her life, spices are my passion today. With

The Spice Merchant's Daughter, I hope to share all that she taught me and enhance the way you cook and eat at home. Just as my mother's spices inspired my own passion for cooking, the recipes that follow will help you bring the flavors of Southeast Asia straight to your table.

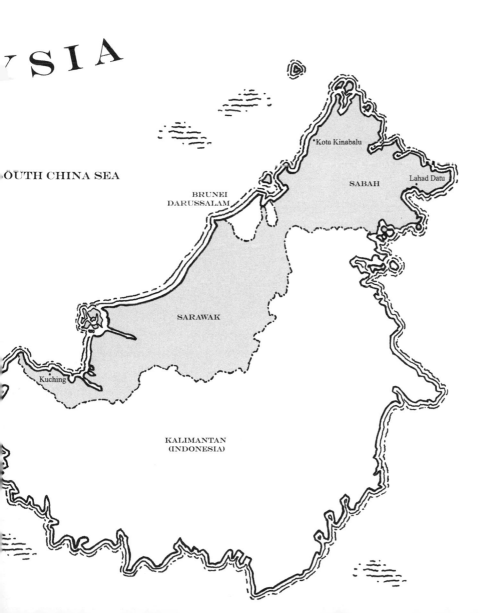

The Spice Pantry

Strategically tucked at the crossroads, the Indian Ocean on the west and the South China Sea on the east, Malacca, on the Straits of the Malay Peninsula, was destined from time immemorial to be the most important trading area in the spice trade. Throughout history, merchants from Arabia, Persia, India, China, and beyond converged at this port, eventually creating a vibrant and bustling marketplace that offered everything from textiles and opium to grains and, of course, spices from around the world. So strong was the influence of spices and so precious was the commodity that some were literally counted grain by grain! The spice cupboards in the homes of those who could afford these luxuries were kept under lock and key.

No longer a rarity, these spices still possess a certain magic to delight the palate and the cook. And although spices and herbs such as dill, rosemary, and caraway are sold in many supermarkets in America, this chapter focuses on the seasonings that are most commonly used in Southeast Asian cooking, starting with those stored in the cupboard and ending with ones stored in the refrigerator.

The Pantry

I have developed a must-have spice and seasoning pantry that enables you to use these spices as the foundation of your cooking to impart wondrous flavors to your food. For the spices, I have also indicated whether they are mild, hot, or aromatic. With this information you can navigate the spice rack at your local supermarket or shop at any Asian store with confidence, knowing exactly what to buy and how to use it. Store spices in clean airtight bottles away from sunlight at room temperature and the spices will keep well for over six months.

Anise (aromatic) BOTANICAL NAME: *PIMPINELLA ANISUM*

Anise seeds are highly fragrant, ⅛ to ⅕ inch long, and have a fine short stalk attached to their greenish brown slightly crescent-shaped seeds. Although they look similar to cumin, you can tell the difference from the shape and licorice aroma. There are many ways to use anise seeds: add ½ teaspoon of anise seeds to hot oil before adding vegetables such as cabbage, cauliflower, zucchini, and potato to give dishes a delicious nutty and savory flavor. Mix anise seeds with cream cheese for dips or spreads or use them in dense bread doughs or in soups. Note that adding too much anise seed will make your dish bitter, however.

Cardamom (aromatic) BOTANICAL NAME: *ELETTARIA CARDAMOMUM*

Cardamom pods, from a shrub in the ginger family, are harvested when green just before they open. They are then sorted meticulously by hand and dried on mats under the sun until they turn a pale green. Crushing the green pods unveils the fragrant black seeds inside. Lightly pound or grind the seeds to a fine powder to add aroma and infuse flavor into rice, curries, tea, and desserts. The recipes in this book call for the use of only green cardamom pods. I do not use white cardamom pods, although available in stores, as they are bleached and not as aromatic.

Chiles, Dried (hot) BOTANICAL NAME: *CAPSICUM*

From a tingle on the tongue to a full-blown explosion, chiles have been adding heat and flavor to food all over the world for centuries. Chiles were relatively unknown to Southeast Asia until the Portuguese traders introduced them to the region in the later part of the sixteenth century. Prior to the availability of chile peppers, peppercorns were used to provide the pungency or "heat" in Southeast Asian cuisine. As a rule of thumb, the smaller the chile, the hotter it is. To reduce the heat of any chile, remove the seeds, which contain 80 percent of a chile's capsaicin, the source of the heat. Once you become used to cooking with chiles, you'll be surprised at the many flavors of different varieties. Some of the dried chiles I use most often are:

DE ÁRBOL—These skinny red chiles are typically 3 or 4 inches long. They are very hot if the seeds are left intact; the chile has a smoky flavor.

NEW MEXICO OR ANAHEIM (sometimes labeled *California*)—These large dark red pods are about 6 inches long and also have a smoky flavor.

JAPONE—Bright red with pods about 3 inches long, these chiles are aromatic, smoky, and peppery in flavor. I normally like to fry them in oil and then reserve the chile oil, which is great for adding instant heat to noodle dishes and soups.

These chiles are commonly found in supermarkets. You may use them interchangeably, depending upon which one is available in your store, when recipes call for dried chiles. Whole dried chiles can be ground into chile powder using a spice grinder (see below). Hot red pepper flakes, or crushed dried chiles, are also widely available. In Southeast Asian cuisine, dried chiles are commonly used to impart a red hue to sambals and spice pastes. The chiles must be cut and soaked in hot water first until softened before being ground into a paste.

Pure Chile Powder or Homemade Cayenne

Making your own chile powder is a wonderful way to preserve the sharp heat and red hue of a chile. Many store-bought chile powders appear red but contain fillers such as mace, sugar, and pepper, which take away the aroma and robust flavor of the chile. By preparing the powder at home, you keep it pure and control the heat you desire. Use de Árbol, New Mexico or Anaheim, or Japone interchangeably. Fill a spice grinder with as many chiles as it will hold. Grind to a fine powder (the texture should be similar to that of ground black pepper). Sift the ground chiles using a fine sieve and place in an airtight glass jar. Use within 3 months.

Cinnamon *(aromatic)* BOTANICAL NAME: *CINNAMOMUM VERUM*

Cinnamon is a small evergreen tree indigenous to Sri Lanka, although today you will find it cultivated on the many spice islands of the Malay Archipelago. The cinnamon tree grows up to 30 feet in height. When you pluck any part of a cinnamon tree, you will note a lovely scent of cinnamon. Cinnamon is obtained by removing the inner and outer bark of the tree. The inner bark curls naturally into quills to form a cylinder. The taste of cinnamon is pungent yet sweet. In Southeast Asian cooking, a few sticks of cinnamon are usually added to hot oil together with other spices and cooked until fragrant before the main ingredients are added. I love the aroma of cinnamon, which is always partnered with star anise to add maximum flavor to meat dishes. Cinnamon sticks are also used whole to flavor hot drinks. During my childhood, cinnamon sticks were coated with sugar and sold as lollipops. Add several sticks of cinnamon to your sugar container and the sugar will pick up hints of cinnamon; you can then use this sugar in baking. Ground cinnamon is best made fresh at home—either in a spice grinder or using a grater—but can also be purchased in stores.

Cloves *(aromatic)* BOTANICAL NAME: *EUGENIA CARYOPHYLLUS* OR *SYZYGIUM AROMATICUM*

The aromatic clove is the unopened flower bud of a pyramid-shaped evergreen tree that reaches up to 50 feet in height. When sun-dried these buds turn brownish black. Cloves have a sweet, earthy, peppery taste, and they pair well with most meat dishes. Quickly rub them between your palms, then lightly fry cloves in a little oil to release their essential oils before adding your main ingredients. Whole cloves taste great with coffee; add two to a cup of coffee to try the combination. You can also grind cloves into a powder for use in spice rubs or in your baking. Grind only small quantities as needed—the flavor and color fade over time.

Coriander *(mild)* BOTANICAL NAME: *CORIANDRUM SATIVUM*

The dried seeds from the cilantro plant (see page 30) are called *coriander*. Coriander seeds are yellowish brown and often used in the preparation of curry powders and other spice rubs. When I prepare curries at home, I like to add some coriander seeds to the hot oil to impart their warm, spicy-aromatic, semisweet taste to the food. In Southeast Asian homes children are introduced to mild curries featuring coriander instead of cayenne. Ground coriander is made from coriander seeds and can be made at home or purchased in stores.

Cumin *(aromatic)* Botanical Name: *Cuminum cyminum*

Cumin seeds, the dried fruit of a small slender annual herb, originated in Egypt and later found their way to Asia through the spice route. The seeds are brown and have a strong, spicy-sweet aroma with a slightly bitter taste. Cumin closely resembles fennel, although the latter is bigger, lighter in appearance, and has an aniselike flavor. Cumin seeds can be added to soups, lentils, curries, and savory rice dishes and pair well with coriander. To make ground cumin, simply crush the seeds into powder in a mortar and pestle or, for larger quantities, use a spice grinder. Sift and store your freshly ground cumin in an airtight glass jar. You can also buy cumin already ground. The pungency and bitterness of cumin are particularly evident in ground form, but toasting the spice brings out a nutty flavor that's less harsh. Ground cumin goes well with seafood and yogurt dishes.

Fennel *(aromatic)* Botanical Name: *Foeniculum vulgare*

Fennel is regarded as one of the sacred herbs in Indian customs. The plant is often hung over doorways to ward off evil spirits and is believed to keep young people strong and healthy. Only the seeds of the fennel plant are used in Southeast Asian cooking, although in the Mediterranean the entire plant is used as an herb and a vegetable. Fennel seeds are grayish green and have a sweet, mellow flavor similar to that of anise seeds. Fennel seeds complement seafood particularly well when a teaspoon of crushed or whole seeds is added to hot oil; allow the spice to sizzle before adding the seafood. Alternatively, you may pound or grind the fennel seeds into powder, add salt, and use as a spice rub for seafood. Ground fennel is less sweet and stronger than whole fennel seeds.

Fenugreek *(aromatic)* Botanical Name: *Trigonella foenum-graecum*

Fenugreek seeds are small, hard, and yellowish brown. In Southeast Asia, the dried seeds are used mainly to flavor seafood curries, lentil soup, pickles, and chutneys. Be sure not to add too much fenugreek as it can overpower the flavors of other spices. Fenugreek seeds have a strong aroma and a slightly bitter, nutty taste. Use 5 to 7 seeds in hot oil, allowing them to sizzle before adding your main ingredient.

Ginger, Ground *(hot)* BOTANICAL NAME: *ZINGIBER OFFICINALE*

When fresh ginger is dried and then milled, you get ground ginger. Typically, in Southeast Asian cuisine, it is used in the preparation of curry masala, in spice rubs, and in baking. Ground ginger has a sharp bite, although it does not have the strong aroma of fresh ginger. Ground ginger is not a good substitute for fresh ginger (see page 32). A good-quality ground ginger is brilliant yellow, not dull beige, and has a mild aroma of ginger.

Lemon Peel, Dried, and Lemon Peel Granules

Dried lemon peel is obtained by grating fresh lemon for its zest and then baking the zest in the oven at 350°F for 20 minutes, until dehydrated. When the zest is baked, it is normal for the bright yellow color to darken slightly. The flavor is citrusy but not harsh. A good substitute is store-bought dried lemon peel, often sold as lemon peel granules. Always check the ingredients list to make sure that lemon peel is the only ingredient listed. The granules should be slightly sweet and have a fruity lemon smell, not a woody scent. You can find the granules at most whole food stores and on the Internet.

Mustard *(hot)* BOTANICAL NAME: *BRASSICA JUNCEA*

Mustard seeds have appeared in Sanskrit records dating as far back as 3000 B.C. There are three types of mustard plants that produce seeds: the black mustard (*Brassica nigra*), pale yellow or white mustard (*Sinapsis alba*) native to Europe, and the tiny, dark reddish brown mustard seeds (*Brassica juncea*) widely used in Southeast Asian cooking. Mustard seeds have a hot and pungent taste and are always cooked in hot oil until they pop to produce a pleasant nutty, sweet flavor. When cooked, mustard seeds can be added to a variety of vegetable and lentil dishes, sauces, and curries. If you want to use them in chutneys and pickles, the seeds should be dry roasted and ground instead. Mustard seeds can also be used in marinades for meat or seafood. Grind about 1 tablespoon of mustard seeds into powder and mix with water to form a paste before adding it to your marinade for a hot, sharp taste. For a milder flavor, mix the seeds into 3 tablespoons of milk and follow the same process.

Nutmeg and Mace (aromatic) BOTANICAL NAME: *MYRISTICA FRAGRANS*

Nutmeg, native to the Banda Islands, is an evergreen tree that grows up to 60 feet and in many areas outside of its indigenous home. The nutmeg tree produces fruits with firm yellow flesh. Inside the fruit is a nut covered by a hard, shiny brown shell called *nutmeg*. The outer portion of the shell consists of a red lacy web known as *mace*. To select a good nutmeg, simply shake it briskly; if it is of high quality, the inner core should move inside. Although supermarkets sell ground nutmeg, in this form it does not contain the volatile oil necessary to provide maximum flavor. Always buy whole nutmeg and grate it only before using. Known as *buah kemiri* in Malaysia and Indonesia, nutmeg is used in making spice paste, to flavor savory dishes, and in desserts. I add a few fresh nutmegs to my sugar bowl. The sugar takes on a lovely aroma of nutmeg, and I use this scented sugar in making desserts.

Paprika (mild) BOTANICAL NAME: *CAPSICUM ANNUM*

Paprika is a bright red powder made from dried sweet chile from the many varieties of *Capsicum annum*. There are several kinds of paprika on the market. The sweet variety is the most common, also known as *Hungarian paprika*. This paprika is bright red in color and can be purchased at grocery stores. When heated, this paprika releases savory-sweet flavor and therefore can be used to flavor lentil and curry dishes or sprinkled over chicken or fish before cooking. There is also hot paprika. If you cannot find it in stores, simply add a dash of cayenne to your recipe instead, to taste. Mild chiles and sweet bell peppers are also smoked to produce smoked paprika, commonly used in making spice rubs, especially for seafood.

Although paprika is seldom used in Southeast Asian cooking, I am fond of this spice for its mild flavor and light aroma. A few dashes of paprika mixed with sea salt and pepper are great on eggs or in salad dressings. Paprika blended with Ginger-Garlic Paste (page 59), some hot red pepper flakes, salt, and olive oil makes a lovely marinade for barbecued meats and roasts. Since paprika becomes bitter with age, always purchase small quantities to get the most out of its unique flavor.

Parsley, Dried (aromatic) BOTANICAL NAME: *UMBELLIFERIA* OR *PETROSELINUM CRISPUM*

Parsley is an upright branched plant with green leaves growing in clusters and belongs to the same family as dill, celery, and parsnip. Although the fresh herb is favored in Mediterranean cooking, it is not used in Southeast Asian cuisine. Instead the leaves and stems are dried and used as culinary flavorings in spice rubs and masalas.

Peppercorns (hot) BOTANICAL NAME: *PIPER NIGRUM*

Pepper comes from a pungent-smelling vine that grows in abundance in the hot tropical regions of mainly Sarawak in East Malaysia. When forming on the vine, pepper berries are green; they turn into black peppercorns when picked and dried under the sun. When the shell is removed from the black peppercorns through a tiresome steaming process, you get white peppercorns. All peppercorns—green, white, and black—come from the same plant. Pepper is an extremely valuable spice in Southeast Asian cooking. You can use black pepper for its piquancy in most dishes. Ground white peppercorns are less aromatic and can be sprinkled on eggs or added to stir-fried rice. Green peppercorns pair well with seafood and are used mostly for stir-fried dishes.

Saffron (aromatic) BOTANICAL NAME: *CROCUS SATIVUS*

Painstakingly harvested by hand, saffron is the stigma of a wild crocus. It is cultivated in Iran, India, and regions of the Mediterranean. It takes nearly an acre to produce one pound of saffron, making it the most expensive spice in the world. When buying saffron, look for a vibrant red, not a dull brick color, which indicates an old crop. The intensive color of saffron comes from carotenoids, and soaking saffron in milk or warm water releases their slightly bitter essential oil and color. Spanish saffron has a sweet taste, while the Iranian and Indian variety offers a savory taste. Use saffron to color your rice dishes, cakes, and other desserts. You can also blend garlic and butter with saffron-infused milk to use as a spread. The best way to store saffron is to wrap it in foil and place in a jar with a tight-fitting lid in a cool dark place.

Star Anise (aromatic) BOTANICAL NAME: *ILLICIUM VERUM*

Star anise is the beige flowerhead of a tree that is a member of the magnolia family. It is popular with the Chinese, who use it liberally in their food. Found throughout Southeast Asia, particularly in Thailand, Malaysia, and Sumatra, star anise is harvested from August to October using hooks attached to a long pole or by shaking the branches. The harvested fruits are dried in the sun until they turn deep reddish brown. Star anise looks like an eight-pointed star, each containing a shiny brownish black seed. Star anise releases an aromatic, sweet taste when cooked. The recipes in this book use star anise in the whole form, not powdered. You can add star anise to meat dishes, soups, and stews for a hearty taste.

Thyme, Dried (aromatic) BOTANICAL NAME: *THYMUS VULGARIS*

There are many varieties of thyme, the most common being the garden variety, which is widely used as a culinary herb and as an herbal medicine. Thyme, fresh or dried, is not used in Southeast Asian cooking, but I have come to love its warm and aromatic flavor and add it to soups, potatoes, and vegetables, especially mushroom and seafood dishes. Dried thyme is a lovely herb suitable for making spice rubs. The flavor is mild, so rub the herb between your fingers to release the aromatic oils before using it.

Turmeric (mild) BOTANICAL NAME: *CURCUMA DOMESTICA*

Part of the ginger family, turmeric is cultivated for its intense flavor and vivid yellow color. The fresh rhizomes of a lily family plant are usually sun-dried and then crushed to make powdered turmeric. Both powdered and the fresh rhizomes are used in Southeast Asian cooking. You may use a pinch of ground turmeric in curries, soups, and rice dishes or sprinkle it on meat and seafood before cooking. The fresh rhizome, available throughout the year, can be crushed for its juice and used to produce a lovely yellow color in rice dishes. Use only a small amount, the size of a pea, or your food will end up bitter. Also take care not to stain your clothing or utensils when cooking with fresh turmeric. Besides in cooking, turmeric is used as a natural coloring in cosmetics and textiles. Orthodox Buddhist monks are known to dye their robes in turmeric because of its antiseptic properties. Fresh turmeric can be purchased at most Asian or Southeast Asian grocery stores.

Toasting Dried Spices

All spices weaken in flavor with time. Ground cardamom loses its flavor in a week, while ground cinnamon stays fresh and fragrant for 3 months. Whole spices are fuller bodied and therefore deteriorate much more slowly than ground spices. This is due to the amount of volatile or natural essential oils that provides the flavor in each spice. Both whole and ground spices benefit from being toasted before using to activate the oils and revive the flavor.

How to Toast Whole Spices

Keep some of the raw spice on a plate next to the stove when you are toasting; this will help you judge the color change. Break heavier or denser spices, such as cinnamon, star anise, and cloves, into pieces before toasting. Put the spices in a dry skillet over medium-low heat and use a wooden spoon to continuously move the spices to avoid burning them. When the spices appear one shade darker and become fragrant, they are done. Immediately remove them and set aside to cool briefly on a plate before grinding them. (Remember, the spices will continue to cook for a few seconds after being removed from the heat.) Lighter spices, such as coriander, cardamom, cumin, fennel, and mustard seed, can be toasted whole.

How to Toast Ground Spices

Commercially processed ground spices are less expensive than whole spices, but they lack the aromatic properties of whole spices as the essential oils that give spices their flavor are lost or oxidized during drying, crushing, grinding, and other processing. You can, however, enhance the flavor of ground spices by placing them in a dry skillet and briefly heating them over medium-low heat, stirring constantly, until fragrant. Ground spices are extremely delicate and will burn quickly if you don't pay close attention to them. Ground spices such as turmeric and paprika are seldom toasted; rather, they are used to add color and health benefits to dishes.

Grinding Dried Spices

In Southeast Asia, home cooks can purchase freshly ground spices at the market daily. Here in America, I rely on the spice grinder or coffee grinder to transform whole spices into aromatic fine powder and use them as needed.

Place lighter spices inside the spice grinder and then any heavier ones on the top and grind them in batches to a fine powder. Using this method will prevent the larger spices from getting caught between the blades. Your spice grinder should be at least half full for best results. Sift the powder before using.

Other Pantry Ingredients
Chana Dal (Yellow Split Peas)

These yellow split peas are a relative of the common chickpea. When toasted they release a slightly sweet taste and nutty flavor and as such I use them in many of my masala recipes. If using them to make lentil dishes, first soak them overnight. They are very nutritious and easy to digest. You can buy them at most Indian grocery stores.

Coconut Milk and Cream

In Southeast Asia, the *monyet,* or male monkeys, are trained to identify the ripe fruit of the tall coconut trees and to harvest about a thousand coconuts a day. Many coconuts are cracked open for their white flesh and sold to local markets, where the vendor grinds the flesh of the coconut to produce fresh coconut milk. No sugar or preservatives are added. In America, I purchase my coconut milk in a can imported from Thailand. When you purchase canned coconut milk, do not shake the can, as the cream is at the top. Scoop out the thick cream and use it when the recipe calls for coconut cream. Use the rest, the thin liquid, as coconut milk. Coconut cream can also be purchased canned on its own at Southeast Asian and gourmet markets. Use this when a recipe calls for more than ¼ cup coconut cream. I am fond of Chao Koh and Mae Ploy brands, which do not have cornstarch added to them. Once the can is opened, transfer the coconut cream or milk to a lidded container and place in the refrigerator for up to 1 week or in the freezer for up to 3 months.

Fish Sauce

Fish sauce is used to add the saltiness that many Southeast Asian dishes require. It is made from small fishes too small to be eaten, often taken from large catches by the net fishing industry. At the factory, these fishes are placed in large containers and covered with a mass quantity of sea salt (about 40 percent of their weight), which will both flavor and preserve the fish. Salt is also added to keep the fish on the bottom of the container during fermentation. The highly concentrated fish sauce is filtered several times, strained, and bottled for the market.

Fish sauce is sold in many grades in Southeast Asia. My personal favorite, and the one that is appreciated by all my cooking students, is the high-quality transparent golden brown liquid sold under the name Golden Boy. It has a pleasant scent and tastes great in my dishes.

Palm Sugar

Palm sugar trees are abundant in Thailand and Malaysia. When the trees are about twenty years old, their sweet sap can be extracted from the young yellow blossoms to make palm sugar. During the harvest the farmer climbs up these sturdy trees and carries with him several bamboo cylinders, where the sap is collected. The raw sap is then filtered and boiled in a very large wok until the sap caramelizes and turns a deep red color. This sap has now been transformed into sweet palm sugar. The palm sugar is placed in molds or into woven palm leaf containers to be sold at nearby markets or exported. It has a delicious caramel flavor and is an important balancing agent in Southeast Asian dishes. Even a very spicy chile dish will lose its intensity with the addition of palm sugar.

Palm sugar is sold in block form, wrapped in plastic packets or in jars, at most Southeast Asian grocery stores in America.

Palm Sugar Syrup
MAKES 1 CUP

To facilitate using a small amount of palm sugar at a time, make liquid palm sugar by cooking an 8-ounce block of palm sugar in ¼ cup water over medium heat until melted, without stirring. The syrup is ready when large bubbles appear on the surface. Let it cool before pouring it into a glass jar. Refrigerate for up to 2 weeks. You may substitute Lyle's Golden Syrup (available at gourmet markets) or brown sugar for palm sugar, although the taste will not be as mellow.

Potato Starch

This gluten-free starch can be found at most supermarkets. In Southeast Asian cuisine, we use it to coat food such as chicken before frying for a crunchy texture. The starch is also great as a thickening agent since it dissolves evenly in sauces and the sauces will also not congeal on cooling.

Soy Sauce

Soy sauce is made from soybeans that have been washed, soaked, and pressure-cooked in large steel vats. Ground wheat and cultures are added to the cooked beans, and after several days of fermentation in a controlled environment, the beans turn greenish and are transferred to tanks and covered in brine to ferment for several more months. The mixture is finally filtered, pasteurized, and bottled as soy sauce. (What does not turn to sauce is sold in the market as "salted beans" or "yellow bean sauce.") There are many types of soy sauces on the market, and trying some new ones can be fun. I prefer to use soy sauce brands that are made in Southeast Asia as they are less salty than many others.

Sweet Soy Sauce *(Kecap Manis)*

Translated as *kecap* (soy) and *manis* (sweet), this dark, thick soy sauce is a much loved seasoning in Southeast Asian cooking. It is flavored with palm sugar, star anise, and garlic and has a distinct molasseslike taste. Use kecap manis to achieve a rich, complex flavor in your dish; even a tablespoon will make a difference in marinades, especially for grilled meats, and in noodle dishes. When buying a good-quality sauce look for ABC brand kecap manis in dark-colored bottles at most Asian grocery stores.

The Refrigerator

In this section I have listed perishable aromatics and ingredients frequently used in Southeast Asian cooking. I recommend that you store the aromatics in a sealed plastic bag or container to extend their freshness. Some ingredients will freeze well for up to 3 months.

Asian Sweet Basil   BOTANICAL NAME: *OCIMUM BASILICUM*

This herb has come to be known as "Thai basil" in America, although it is consumed abundantly throughout Southeast Asia and is referred to there as *Asian sweet basil.* This basil has a texture more delicate than that of regular basil and a sweet licorice aroma. The dark green leaves of this plant grow on purplish stems and are intensely aromatic. In Southeast Asian cuisine, we enjoy basil for its sweet anise flavor and add it to salads, soups, stir-fries, and curries. It is available year-round, and you will find it wrapped in plastic in the herb section of most Asian markets, many gourmet markets, and some farmers' markets. Before using, rub the leaves gently between your palms to release their scent. Always wrap the basil in paper towels and then plastic wrap before refrigerating.

Candlenuts BOTANICAL NAME: *ALEURITES MOLUCCANA*

Native to Malaysia and Indonesia, the candlenut tree grows up to 50 feet and produces small white flowers that grow in clusters at the end of branches. The fruits from the flowers are called *candlenuts.* Candlenuts, known as *biji kemiri* in Indonesian, are round, waxy, and cream colored and are related to the macadamia nut. The nut has an oily consistency and when pounded into a paste adds texture and a delicate flavor to seafood dishes. Candlenuts can be found at most Southeast Asian grocery stores or even Mexican markets. **Never** eat candlenuts raw as they cause stomach disorders. Use macadamia nuts as a substitute.

Chiles, Fresh BOTANICAL NAME: *CAPSICUM*

Like dried chiles (see page 16), fresh chiles are used abundantly in Southeast Asian recipes to add fire and flavor. These are the three varieties, all widely available at supermarkets, that I turn to most in America:

JALAPEÑO—This fleshy chile comes in both green and red and ranges from mild to medium heat. When recipes in this book call for fresh red or green chiles without naming a particular variety, use jalapeños.

BIRD'S-EYE—This chile is about 2 inches long, contains lots of seeds, and is very hot. It comes in both green and red. In Malaysia we call it *chili padi,* and in Thai it is referred to as *prik kee nu.* This chile is also known to many as "Thai chile."

SERRANO—Easily found in most supermarkets, this chile is about 2 inches long, bright to dark green in color when young, and yellow, orange, scarlet, or brown when ripe. It is bullet-shaped with thick flesh and has a crisp, hot taste. Serranos make a good substitute for fresh bird's-eye chiles. When buying, select chiles that are firm to the touch.

Chopped chiles and chiles ground to paste can be stored in containers in the refrigerator for 1 week to expedite cooking preparation. Whole chiles will freeze in freezer bags for 3 months or more.

Cilantro BOTANICAL NAME: *CORIANDRUM SATIVUM*

Cilantro—with its distinctive aroma and warm, sweet, and fruity flavor—is probably the most commonly used herb in Southeast Asia, where the entire plant is used in cooking. The roots have the greatest concentration of flavor, but if the roots are unavailable, you can use the stems instead. Use the tender leaves for flavoring curries and soups, in salads, and for making chutneys, stirring it in at the end. Store cilantro wrapped in a paper towel and then plastic wrap. Cilantro stems and roots will freeze well in freezer bags for up to 3 months.

Curry Leaf BOTANICAL NAME: *MURRAYA KOENIGII*

Nearly every Malaysian Indian home has a curry leaf tree in its yard. The plant was brought by Indian migrants in the fifteenth century and initially planted on temple grounds. The small leaves, also known as *daun kari,* have a distinctive fragrance similar to anise and are used for making curry powders, chutneys, and pickles. In cooking, especially for curries, the flavor of the leaves is maximized by frying them in oil with other spices before the main ingredient is added. Curry leaves pair well with potatoes, seafood, and meat dishes. You can purchase them packed in plastic bags at most Indian or Southeast Asian grocery stores. Before storing, wrap curry leaves in cheesecloth or paper towels and they will keep for up to 2 weeks in the refrigerator. Do not freeze curry leaves; it diminishes the robust flavor. Curry leaves can be eaten raw or cooked. There is no true substitute for curry leaves.

Galangal BOTANICAL NAME: *ALPINIA GALANGA*

Native to Indonesia and the Malay Peninsula, galangal is a member of the ginger family with a unique pungency and sweet aroma. Used in all Southeast Asian cuisine, galangal is commonly pounded with other fresh aromatics such as onions, garlic, and lemongrass to form a spice paste for cooking meat and seafood. You may also add a few slices of galangal to soups and stir-fries for a lovely fragrance and texture. In Malaysia, fresh galangal and its flowers are cut into thin slices and served with a sambal as an appetizer. Galangal can be found at most Southeast Asian grocery stores. Wrapped in a paper towel and stored in the vegetable compartment of the fridge, it can last for up to 2 weeks. You can also slice galangal and freeze it in airtight bags for up to 1 month. This method makes it effortless to remove the quantity you need without having to thaw the whole rhizome.

Garlic BOTANICAL NAME: *ALLIUM SATIVUM*

Garlic belongs to the same family as onions, leeks, and spring onions, which all originate in Central Asia. Heads of garlic sold at many Southeast Asian grocery stores have purple streaks on them and are stronger in flavor than the white-skinned variety. This garlic is also half the size of the ones sold at most Western supermarkets. You may use either variety for recipes in this book. When stir-frying garlic, make sure to cook it until it is golden brown; otherwise you'll end up with a harsh raw garlic taste. To speed up daily cooking preparation, I mince enough fresh garlic for 3 days and store it in an airtight glass jar in the refrigerator.

Garlic Oil

Use this cooked garlic and oil as a garnish for salads.

MAKES ¼ CUP

Heat a small skillet over medium heat for 40 seconds and then add 3 tablespoons peanut oil. Add 1 tablespoon minced garlic and cook for about 30 seconds, until golden. Remove from the heat. Store in an airtight container in the refrigerator for up to 1 week. Serve at room temperature.

Ginger BOTANICAL NAME: *ZINGIBER OFFICINALE*

There are about four hundred types of ginger. Young ginger, which is pale yellow in color with a thin skin that need not be removed, can be eaten raw, pickled, or used in marinades. When recipes in this book call for ginger, use mature ginger, which is beige-brown with a thicker skin that must be peeled. Mature ginger has a wonderfully sweet, warm, and citruslike aroma and a powerful protein-digesting enzyme called *zingibain*. For this reason it is often used as a natural meat tenderizer. You can also use ginger in stir-fries, soups, and curries. The more you grate or chop the ginger the stronger its flavor will be. If you prefer a mild flavor, cut it into large chunks instead. When buying ginger, choose pieces that are firm with shiny unwrinkled skin for best flavor. Wrapped in plastic wrap, it will keep fresh for up to 10 days in the refrigerator. For a longer shelf life (about 3 months), grind the ginger, place in a glass jar, and freeze.

Ginger Tea

When I am down with a cold or flu, I make this warm ginger tea and drink it throughout the day. I always feel so much better afterward.

MAKES 5 CUPS

Bring 1 to 2 tablespoons grated fresh ginger and 5 cups water to a boil in a medium pan. Lower the heat and simmer for 20 minutes. Strain and add 3 tablespoons fresh lemon juice and honey to taste.

Kaffir Lime Leaf BOTANICAL NAME: *CITRUS HYSTRIX*

The kaffir lime has a dark green rough-textured skin and does not contain any juice but releases an intense flavor when grated. In Southeast Asia, the zest is added to soups and desserts. The leaves are also added to soups and, when finely sliced, are great in salads, seafood stir-fries, and curry pastes. If soaking cut fruits or vegetables in water, add a few fresh kaffir lime leaves to help prevent discoloration. The double leaf of the kaffir lime is packed in plastic bags and is available at most Southeast Asian grocery stores. Kaffir lime leaves can be placed in a freezer bag and frozen for up to 2 months. Soak them in water for 5 minutes before using. There is no true substitute for kaffir lime leaves.

Lemongrass BOTANICAL NAME: *CYMBOPOGON CITRATUS*

Lemongrass, a perennial grass that grows up to 3 feet, has bulbs that, when crushed, release a lemony aroma. In Southeast Asia, lemongrass is often planted in backyard gardens for use as a culinary herb and spice. The distinctive lemon-like flavor of lemongrass is strongest 4 inches from the base of the stalk. Lemongrass can be finely sliced, added to salads and stir-fries, or bruised and chopped for use in soups or stocks. Lemongrass is also pounded with other fresh spices to make spice pastes for curry dishes. It can be found at well-stocked supermarkets and gourmet markets. Wrap lemongrass in a paper towel and store it in the vegetable compartment of the fridge for up to 2 weeks. To freeze lemongrass, first grind it with some water or slice it finely, then place in a container and freeze for up to 3 months. To thaw the amount you require, leave it out at room temperature, then use what you need and freeze the remainder. It will not turn rancid provided you use a clean spoon. There is no substitute for lemongrass.

Oyster Sauce

This sauce combines oysters with sugar, salt, wheat flour, cornstarch, caramel, and filtered water boiled together for a few hours in a large steamer until thickened. The sauce is then filtered several times to minimize bacterial contamination, bottled while still hot, and vacuum packed. A good-quality oyster sauce should be dark brown and velvety. Use this sauce to add flavor when stir-frying vegetables, meat, or noodles. The sauce, which should be kept refrigerated once opened, also makes a delicious marinade.

Pandan BOTANICAL NAME: *PANDANUS*

An aromatic member of the screwpine family, the pandan plant has light green oblong leaves and is commonly grown in backyard gardens in Southeast Asia. The flavor is aromatic and sweet and is as important to Asian cuisine as vanilla is to Western food. The pandan leaf is amazingly versatile. Throughout Southeast Asia, the leaf is tied into a knot and added to rice before cooking to provide a fragrance of newly harvested grain. The leaves are also pounded and the juice extracted to flavor and color cakes and sweet coconut puddings. Use it to wrap marinated chicken pieces prior to placing on the grill for great taste. In America, you can buy pandan extract for desserts and fresh or frozen leaves at most Southeast Asian stores. Place the leaves in freezer bags and freeze for up to 3 months. The leaves thaw out quickly under running water.

Shallots BOTANICAL NAME: *ALLIUM ASCALONICUM*

The shallots sold at Southeast Asian grocery stores have a reddish purple skin and are about 1 inch in size. They are also sweeter in flavor and more intense than the larger variety most supermarkets carry. I prefer shallots over onions as they are more aromatic and contain less moisture. In Malaysia, shallots are used daily to make a spicy paste known as *rempah*. Shallots are also fried in oil until crisp and used as a garnish for soups, salads, noodles, and rice dishes. Place sliced shallots in a sealed plastic container lined with paper towels to absorb moisture and store in the refrigerator. The shallots will stay fresh for up to a week. Whole shallots can be kept in the pantry.

Shrimp Paste

Fishermen in the Straits of Malacca and on the island of Penang catch *geragau*, tiny shrimp, using a special fine net spread between two crossed stakes. When the nets are full, the tiny shrimp are rinsed in sea water and placed on stretched mats on the beach to dry. Once dried, the shrimp are mixed with salt and sun-dried again for 8 hours. They are then crushed into a paste and dried on large wooden trays for 2 weeks. The crushing and drying are repeated from time to time to prevent the paste from spoiling. Finally the paste is shaped (usually into blocks), sun-dried again, and packed for the market.

Shrimp paste is called *belachan* in Malaysia, *trassi* in Indonesia, and *kapi* in Thailand and pairs well with chile dishes; its strong smell dissipates when it is mixed with other ingredients. Available in block form or in tubs, shrimp paste is naturally dark brown in color but you may also find it chemically dyed a deep pink. I always purchase the shrimp paste without the dye as the taste is far superior. Given the high salt content, shrimp paste has a long shelf life. The paste should be wrapped in foil and placed in an airtight bag before being refrigerated.

It's important to note that when you purchase shrimp paste, it is raw and must be cooked in the recipe or toasted before use. To toast, spoon the shrimp paste onto a doubled square of aluminum foil and bake in a 350°F oven for 15 to 20 minutes.

Tamarind

The tamarind tree is more than just an ornamental tree that provides shade from the scorching tropical sun. Whenever I return home to Malaysia, I enjoy plucking the gnarled tamarind pods and savoring the fruity, soft brown pulp inside by coating it in sugar—it tastes like sweet and sour candy. When tamarind pulp is diluted in water, the liquid is used in curries, chutneys, soups, and noodle dishes such as pad thai. Mix tamarind liquid with pantry ingredients or spice paste to add a welcome twang to marinades. For example, tamarind liquid mixed with Ginger-Garlic Paste (page 59) and coconut milk makes a lovely marinade for seafood. Tamarind is sold in 14-ounce blocks at most Asian shops and should be kept refrigerated. The block is not used in cooking until it has broken down into liquid form. Whenever tamarind liquid is called for in this book, use this recipe.

Tamarind Liquid

MAKES 2 CUPS

Put half of a 14-ounce block of tamarind in a medium bowl. Add 2½ cups hot water and allow the tamarind to sit for 10 minutes to soften. Using your fingers, squeeze the tamarind block (like you would squeeze a sponge) until the pulp separates from the seeds and dissolves in the water. Strain the tamarind liquid into a medium bowl. Discard any seeds and pulp that have not dissolved. The strained tamarind liquid should be reddish brown. Store tamarind liquid in the refrigerator for up to 1 week or in the freezer for up to 3 months.

Pounding Fresh Aromatics

Ingredients such as galangal, fresh ginger and turmeric, lemongrass, onions, shallots, garlic, and fresh chiles in various combinations form the foundation of curry pastes. There are multiple ways to transform these fresh aromatics into a well-balanced paste. The traditional method, still the best, is to use a heavy stone mortar and pestle. This method, used for centuries throughout Southeast Asia, produces a remarkably perfumed paste with deep flavor. The heavy grayish green mortar can be found at most Southeast Asian grocery stores.

If you wish to use the mortar and pestle, here are some straight-forward guidelines to follow: First peel, slice, or chop all the ingredients into smaller pieces. Begin by adding hard and fibrous ingredients such as lemongrass, galangal, or candlenuts to the mortar, one at a time. Strike with a strong up-and-down movement, aiming directly at the spice in the mortar. The idea is to break down the fibers and release the essential oils in each ingredient. You may add some sea salt to assist in your pounding. As you pound, bring the ingredients to the center of the mortar so that they will be ground to a uniform texture. Next, add the softer ingredients such as ginger, turmeric, and fresh or reconstituted dried chiles. These should be crushed to a fine paste before you add ingredients that contain more moisture such as shallots, garlic, lime, and cilantro leaves. The latter will be broken down easily by pounding and are prone to splatter, and for those reasons they are added toward the end.

When pressed for time between work and kids, I truly appreciate the convenience of a food processor or mini-chopper. I first crush my ingredients a little using a mortar and a pestle, just to release their essential oils, then put everything in a food processor or mini-chopper and blend with a little water until I have a smooth paste. If you are going to fry your spice paste, add a little oil to the food processor instead of water. If you are going to simmer the paste in coconut milk, you can add that liquid instead.

The Healing Power of Herbs and Spices

Many families in Southeast Asia believe that herbs and spices alleviate various ailments. This is why—in addition to their flavor-enhancing properties—these ingredients factor so strongly into the region's cooking. Here are some of the ways they are used, along with their supposed health benefits:

ANISE: Add a pinch of anise seeds to yogurt to aid digestion.

BASIL: Steep a few sprigs of basil in a cup of hot water and drink to aid digestion and for its antioxidant properties.

CARDAMOM: Add ¼ teaspoon cardamom seeds to your warm cup of tea to aid digestion. Chew 3 to 4 cardamom pods to relieve coughing.

CHILES: Eat dishes rich in chiles to lose weight.

CINNAMON: Put cinnamon in your next cup of tea to relieve a cough. High in antioxidants, cinnamon is also believed to lower cholesterol.

CLOVES: Steep 5 cloves in warm water and drink the water to get rid of body odor.

CORIANDER: Mix ½ teaspoon crushed seeds with warm water and consume to help alleviate nausea and vomiting.

CUMIN: Steep ½ teaspoon cumin in a cup of water and drink to reduce flatulence.

FENNEL SEEDS: Chew on fennel seeds to freshen breath and aid digestion.

FENUGREEK: Soak ½ teaspoon fenugreek seeds in water overnight and drink to help reduce cholesterol.

GALANGAL: Boil galangal in water and drink to improve digestion. You can mix powdered galangal with honey to treat coughs.

GARLIC: Crush 2 garlic cloves and eat raw with a teaspoon of honey to help lower cholesterol.

(continued)

Ginger: Add a few slices of ginger to your tea to stimulate appetite, improve circulation, and relieve nausea.

Lemongrass: Bruise the bulbs and boil them in water to treat stomachaches and flatulence. It is also a wonderful tonic against colds.

Nutmeg: Add ½ teaspoon freshly grated nutmeg to your cup of coffee or tea to treat indigestion and stomachaches.

Peppercorns: Grind ¼ cup peppercorns with ¼ cup olive oil or coconut oil in a food processor to make a paste. Apply as a body scrub to promote blood circulation and keep the body warm. Alternatively, boil 1 teaspoon black peppercorns with 1½ cups water and 1 teaspoon honey over medium heat for 15 minutes. Strain and drink. Consumed in food, pepper stimulates the appetite and aids digestion.

Star anise: Add 2 star anise to your cup of tea to treat flatulence.

Tamarind: Drink a glass of warm tamarind water mixed with 1 teaspoon honey to relieve an upset stomach.

Thyme: Steep a few sprigs of thyme in a cup of hot water and drink to help relieve coughing.

Turmeric: Sprinkle turmeric on cuts and wounds as an antiseptic powder or mix with milk to settle the stomach.

Merchant's Curry Powders, Rubs, Spice Pastes, and Sauces

Basic Curry Powder
Quick Curry Powder
Merchant's Garam Masala
Fiery Curry Powder for Meat
Korma Masala
Curry Powder for Fish

✦

Lemon Pepper Rub
Steak and Chop Rub
Green Seafood Rub

✦

Traditional Sambal
Thai Red Curry Paste
Thai Green Curry Paste
Thai Massaman Curry Paste
Ginger-Garlic Paste
Cilantro-Garlic Paste
Roasted Chile Paste
Seafood Spice Paste
Chicken Spice Paste

✦

Sweet-Sour Sauce
Perfect Peanut Sauce
Merchant's Barbecue Sauce

"Aunty! Aunty!" our neighbor would call out to my mother over the low chain-link fence that separated our homes. The two women would share a daily ritual, discussing what they were cooking. In the backyard, close to the kitchen, we grew herbs and spices for our daily needs. As a little girl, I would eagerly tail my mother on her morning venture into our spice garden, a warm tapestry of colors, textures, and scents engulfing my young senses. It was my retreat, a Shangri-La where my imagination danced with the flowers of the tamarind tree as they fell spinning to the ground.

I would gaze at my mother as she carefully pulled back the dark fragrant leaves of the ginger plant to lift its fresh rhizome and place it in her little rattan basket. Part of the fresh ginger would be used in cooking and the rest added to my mother's hot bath to relieve muscle aches and invigorate the body. If I had had my way, though, my mother would have used it all to make my favorite ginger candy treats. Next, she would proceed to the galangal, a pale cream, flavorful, and more potent rhizome than mature ginger. My mother would then collect some yellow turmeric roots and leaves and some chiles.

"These chiles," my mother would say, "are rich in vitamin C and contain antioxidants." She would pluck them delicately and compare them to Chinese firecrackers due to their bright red color. She also grew green bird's-eye chiles. In my young mind, the chiles resembled the green and red lights on a Christmas tree.

Wending her way back to the kitchen, my mother would pick several aromatic pandan leaves, curry leaves, cilantro, kaffir lime leaves, and a few stalks of lemongrass, adding to her treasures in the basket. Once inside, wiping away the sweat from her brow, she would prepare herself a glass of *kunyit asin* tea, an herbal brew made with ginger, turmeric, and honey, and a rice pancake topped with sweetened coconut milk for me.

A shrill beep from the roving van of the "kicap man," the street-to-street soy sauce seller, would jolt us momentarily. We joined the stream of home cooks who had interrupted their chores to purchase the sauces—sweet soy, light soy, chile, roasted honey, hoisin, and oyster. Sesame oil, soybean paste, and other marinades were also available.

Often our purchases were recorded in a little tattered notebook and the bill settled at the end of the month.

Back in the kitchen, my mother would remove the fresh herbs and spices from her basket and place them on a dark, worn wooden tray. I would wash the chiles, kaffir lime leaves, and lemongrass and peel the shallots, ginger, galangal, and turmeric. My mother would then pound them in our old stone mortar. The garlic was never peeled; Mother said there was no need for fussy refinements, and its skin would fall off when it cooked.

From the kitchen would waft a lovely fragrance that permeated the neighborhood as Mother created an aromatic paste. The fish, bought fresh from the fishmonger, was cleaned and seasoned with turmeric and salt and then fried in hot oil. Later we would toss the fish into a wok with sambal, which would enhance its flavor and crispness.

My mother would wash the lentils, which we would cook with tomatoes, ground turmeric, salt, tamarind, garlic, and water. Several sprigs of curry leaves would be combined with mustard seeds and dried chiles in a little hot oil and added at the last minute to maximize the flavors of the curry leaves in the dal. Sometimes our neighbor would come to our house with ingredients in a baking tray and ask my mother to make dal for her. I still find my mom's dal the tastiest I've ever eaten.

Then some chicken would be minced into a paste with a cleaver and mixed with sweet soy sauce, oyster sauce, Cilantro-Garlic Paste, and a pinch of salt. A large spoonful of this mixture was placed on a pandan leaf, wrapped carefully, then secured with a slender bamboo skewer and fried. We prepared several stuffed pandan leaves, more than enough for the whole family. Several leaves would also be added to jasmine rice before cooking to give the rice a delicious flavor and the lovely fragrance of newly harvested grain.

That day's vegetable dish would be green beans to accompany the rice. Some strong-smelling *belachan,* or shrimp paste, was toasted, then mixed with Roasted Chile Paste and stir-fried with the beans.

All these dishes were then set on the table for our family to feast upon. No matter how simple a family meal, the fresh ingredients in it supplied the nutrition we needed to keep us going, and the real fun was enjoying the sumptuous food together as a family.

My practical approach of preparing all spice pastes, sauces, and marinades in advance allows me to enjoy a variety of dishes without the fuss of chopping and grinding daily for each meal. I rely on these natural flavor enhancers to accentuate the taste of the main ingredients. Most of these spice pastes will keep for up to 1 week in the refrigerator or for longer in the freezer.

Memories of my walks with my mother in her spice garden and the aroma of my mother's home-cooked meals are ever present in my mind, and I eagerly share her cooking style in my own cooking lessons. Over the years, I have taught many people how to employ spices in their cooking without overpowering their dishes. I hope the recipes in this chapter will enable you to do the same, empowering you to create your own masalas, spice rubs, pastes, and sauces so that you can choose just the right flavor and heat for the dishes you prepare.

Curry Powders or Masalas Curry powder, a blend of several pure spices, is also known as *masala*. Most curry powders begin with dried whole spices such as coriander, black peppercorns, cumin, dried chiles, and cardamom pods that are ground and mixed with ground spices like turmeric and ginger. In Southeast Asian cooking, a tablespoon or two of curry powder is combined with fresh aromatics to create a spice-enriched dish. You may choose to add the curry powder either at the beginning or somewhere midpoint of your cooking to make it milder in flavor. You may also combine a tablespoon of curry powder with sauces to make versatile marinades.

An assortment of preblended curry powders is on the market for meat, seafood, poultry, and vegetables. Just as each main ingredient offers a different taste, so do the accompanying curry powders. There are many reasons to make your own curry powder, however. Commercial mixes, although convenient, can lack freshness, flavor, and aroma. Most whole spices retain their essential oils for some time and have a longer shelf life, so purchase spices whole and grind them to create your own home-style curry powder. Once you are proficient, you can custom-blend and adjust the spicing in the curry powder to suit your own palate and without having to use large batches of spice mixes bought from grocery stores. For me, blending my own spices keeps me connected to the days when I was a little girl watching my mother at the mill. I am now creating the same bond with my children and teaching them the fascinating art of blending spices.

Merchant's
Curry
Powders,
Rubs,
Spice
Pastes,
and Sauces
43

Basic Curry Powder

Different curry powders are like building blocks highlighting the flavors of various spices in the cupboard. This basic recipe smells of freshly roasted spices, with the sweet scent of cardamom predominating slightly. It will outshine any curry powder bought from the store.

MAKES ABOUT 1 CUP

20 GREEN CARDAMOM PODS OR
1½ TEASPOONS CARDAMOM SEEDS

TWO 3-INCH CINNAMON STICKS, CRUSHED

1 TABLESPOON BLACK PEPPERCORNS

1 STAR ANISE, CRUSHED

1 TEASPOON CLOVES

¼ CUP CORIANDER SEEDS

2 TABLESPOONS CUMIN SEEDS

1 TABLESPOON ANISE SEEDS

1 TABLESPOON FENNEL SEEDS

2 TEASPOONS FENUGREEK SEEDS

5 DRIED RED CHILES, BROKEN INTO SMALL PIECES

1 TEASPOON GROUND GINGER

1 TABLESPOON GROUND TURMERIC

1. Combine the cardamom, cinnamon, peppercorns, star anise, and cloves in a small skillet over medium-low heat. Cook the spices until fragrant, about 7 minutes. Remove and set aside on a plate to cool.

2. To the same pan, add the coriander, cumin, anise, fennel, and fenugreek seeds and cook over medium heat for 5 minutes, until they release a fragrant scent and become slightly darker, making sure the spices do not turn black. Transfer the spices to a plate to cool.

3. Combine the chiles, ground ginger, ground turmeric, and the toasted spices in a coffee or spice grinder and grind into a fine powder. Allow the ground spices to cool completely before placing in an airtight glass jar. Store in a cool, dry place away from sunlight. Use within 3 months.

Quick Curry Powder Here is an easy way to create a lovely home-style curry using an array of ground spices you may already have in your pantry, eliminating the grinding process. If you are a beginner to curry, you will appreciate this recipe for its mild flavors and ease of preparation. My kids love curry but not its heat, so they especially like this recipe.

If you are not using the curry leaves, omit the oil and start at step 2.

MAKES ABOUT ½ CUP

1 TABLESPOON VEGETABLE OIL

2 SPRIGS FRESH CURRY LEAVES, FINELY CHOPPED (OPTIONAL)

3 TABLESPOONS GROUND CORIANDER

2 TABLESPOONS GROUND CUMIN

2 TEASPOONS GROUND FENNEL

2 TEASPOONS GROUND GINGER

2 TEASPOONS FRESHLY GROUND BLACK PEPPER

1 TEASPOON PURE CHILE POWDER (PAGE 17) OR CAYENNE

½ TEASPOON GROUND CARDAMOM

1 TABLESPOON GROUND TURMERIC

1. Heat the oil in a small skillet over medium heat. Add the curry leaves and fry for 2 minutes or until fragrant. Remove and set aside on a plate to cool.

2. Combine the ground coriander, cumin, fennel, ginger, pepper, chile powder, and cardamom in a separate skillet over medium-low heat. Cook, stirring continuously, until fragrant. This will only take a few seconds since the ground spices will burn easily. Remove from the heat and set aside to cool at room temperature.

3. Combine the curry leaves, toasted spices, and turmeric in a bowl and stir with a spoon until well mixed. Transfer to an airtight glass jar and store in a cool, dry place away from sunlight. Use within 2 months.

Merchant's Garam Masala This is my family's recipe for garam ("warming") masala ("combination of dry-roasted spices"). *Garam* is used to describe spices like cardamom, cloves, and cinnamon that have a warming effect on the body. Add a pinch of garam masala to curries, stews, and stock toward the end of cooking and to potato salads for robust flavor. You may also combine garam masala with Southeast Asian sauces like soy, kecap manis, and oyster to make spice marinades for chicken, pork, and lamb dishes to build layers of flavors. MAKES ABOUT ½ CUP

1 TEASPOON CORIANDER SEEDS

1 TEASPOON BLACK PEPPERCORNS

3 TABLESPOONS GREEN CARDAMOM PODS

2 TABLESPOONS CUMIN SEEDS

¼ CUP CLOVES

FIVE 4-INCH CINNAMON STICKS, BROKEN INTO SMALL PIECES

1 TEASPOON FRESHLY GRATED NUTMEG

1. Combine the coriander, peppercorns, cardamom, cumin, cloves, and cinnamon in a small skillet over medium-low heat. Cook for 7 minutes, stirring constantly to prevent the spices from burning, until the spices release a fragrant scent and become slightly darker, making sure they do not turn black. If they do, it means you have burned them and you will need to start over. Transfer the spices to a plate to cool for 2 to 3 minutes.

2. Combine the toasted spices and nutmeg in a coffee or spice grinder. Grind the spices into a fine powder. Place the garam masala in an airtight glass jar and store in a cool, dry place away from sunlight. Use within 2 months.

Fiery Curry Powder for Meat

If you enjoy your curries spicy, you'll love this recipe. Most Southeast Asian cooks know that a basic curry powder is just not enough to draw the flavors out of meat or chicken. The pungency and heat of spices like chiles, coriander, and black peppercorns are often needed. You may tone this recipe down, however, by using only half the amount of chiles. Use this curry powder in place of cayenne or Basic Curry Powder (page 44) if you like. MAKES ABOUT ⅔ CUP

ONE 3-INCH CINNAMON STICK, CRUSHED	1½ TEASPOONS BLACK PEPPERCORNS
1½ TEASPOONS CLOVES	½ CUP CORIANDER SEEDS
1½ TEASPOONS GREEN CARDAMOM PODS, CRUSHED	1 TABLESPOON CUMIN SEEDS
	1 TABLESPOON FENNEL SEEDS
1 CUP DRIED RED CHILES, BROKEN INTO SMALL PIECES, OR TO TASTE	¼ TEASPOON GROUND TURMERIC

1. Combine the cinnamon, cloves, cardamom, chiles, and peppercorns in a small skillet over medium-low heat. Cook for 7 minutes, until fragrant. Remove and set aside on a plate to cool.

2. Next add the coriander, cumin, and fennel to the pan. Cook until the seeds release a fragrant scent and become slightly darker, about 5 minutes, making sure the spices do not turn black. Transfer the spices to a plate to cool.

3. Combine the toasted spices and the turmeric in a coffee or spice grinder and grind into a fine powder. Allow the ground spices to cool completely. Sift the ground spices and place in an airtight glass jar. Store in a cool, dry place away from sunlight. Use within 3 months.

Korma Masala This is the second most popular masala (after chile powder) in Malaysia, and the spice mills are always busy grinding this masala to meet the demands of home cooks and restaurants. I make it with cinnamon, fennel, and cardamom, which—when ground with cashews and lentils—deliver a creamy, delicately flavored masala similar in color to the light gray-green of ground coriander. The key to this recipe is to keep the cashews light brown without overcooking them. Add this masala to vegetables, potatoes, chicken, or lamb to produce a mild and delicious curry. This masala will still be intensely aromatic after 2 or more months of storage. MAKES ABOUT ⅔ CUP

10 RAW CASHEWS, CRUSHED

1 TABLESPOON YELLOW LENTILS
(CHANA DAL)

ONE 2-INCH CINNAMON STICK, CRUSHED

3 CLOVES

1 TABLESPOON CORIANDER SEEDS

2 TEASPOONS WHITE PEPPERCORNS

1½ TEASPOONS GROUND FENNEL

1 TEASPOON CUMIN SEEDS

1 TEASPOON ANISE SEEDS

½ TEASPOON CARDAMOM SEEDS

1. Combine the cashews with the yellow lentils in a small skillet over medium-low heat. Cook, stirring often, until the cashews are light brown, about 12 minutes. Remove from the pan and set aside on a plate to cool.

2. Now add the cinnamon, cloves, coriander, peppercorns, fennel, cumin, anise, and cardamom to the pan and cook until fragrant, 5 to 7 minutes, taking care not to burn the spices. Set aside on a plate to cool.

3. Put all the ingredients in a coffee or spice grinder. Grind the spices into a fine powder. Allow the ground spices to cool completely. Sift the ground spices and place in an airtight glass jar. Store in a cool, dry place away from sunlight. Use within 3 months.

Curry Powder for Fish Spices like fennel, fenugreek, and coriander when ground have a sweetness and nuttiness that complement the delicate flavor of fish. But for me, they do not provide multilayered flavor when used on their own. Therefore, I add dried chiles and black pepper to give the curry powder a little kick without overpowering the aromatic spices; the chiles also give the curry powder a pleasant orange hue. You may reduce the amount of chiles by half for less heat if you wish. For a quick dinner, combine a tablespoon of this curry powder with salt and olive oil and use as a spice rub on salmon, tuna, halibut, snapper, haddock, or tilapia. Then panfry, bake, or broil the fish. When a recipe in the seafood chapter calls for cayenne or red curry paste, you can use a tablespoon of this curry powder as a substitute. MAKES ABOUT 1½ CUPS

¾ CUP FENNEL SEEDS

½ CUP CORIANDER SEEDS

¼ CUP ROUGHLY BROKEN DRIED RED CHILES

1½ TEASPOONS CUMIN SEEDS

1½ TEASPOONS YELLOW LENTILS (CHANA DAL)

½ TEASPOON BLACK PEPPERCORNS

½ TEASPOON FENUGREEK SEEDS

1. Combine the fennel, coriander, chiles, cumin, lentils, peppercorns, and fenugreek in a medium skillet over medium-low heat. Cook, stirring often, for 15 minutes, until fragrant. Remove and set aside on a plate to cool.

2. Put the spices in a coffee or spice grinder and grind into a fine powder. Allow the ground spices to cool completely. Sift the ground spices and place in an airtight glass jar. Store in a cool, dry place away from sunlight. Use within 3 months.

Merchant's
Curry
Powders,
Rubs,
Spice
Pastes,
and Sauces
49

Spice Rubs Unlike curry powders, rubs are a concentrated blend of a combination of spices (whole and ground) and herbs that add flavor and texture to meat and seafood. Spices such as black peppercorns, coriander seeds, fennel seeds, ground ginger, turmeric, and chiles and dried herbs like thyme, parsley, and mint are some of my favorite ingredients to use in rubs. Salt or garlic salt plays an important role too, as it helps the flavors penetrate the meat. In most of my family recipes, sugar is used minimally, but you may add more to suit your taste.

There are many ways to use spice rubs: Sprinkle them over meats and combine them with vinegar, fresh lemon juice, wine, or yogurt and marinate in the refrigerator as long as overnight to impart flavor and to tenderize. Then bake or grill the meat. Combined with ketchup, molasses, Worcestershire, and vinegar, rubs make lovely barbecue sauces for ribs. And, of course, you can use them to rub all over meat or fish before grilling to provide an instant hit of flavor.

Lemon Pepper Rub This is an exciting, simple-to-make spice mixture that offers a wonderful lemon aroma, a bite from black peppercorns (the king of spices), and a mild sweet flavor from the coriander. It takes just a few tablespoons of this rub on poultry, steak, lamb chops, grilled swordfish kebabs, or potatoes to transform your simplest meals into fresh and peppery delights.

MAKES ABOUT ½ CUP

½ CUP BLACK PEPPERCORNS

2 TABLESPOONS CORIANDER SEEDS

2 TABLESPOONS SALT

2 TABLESPOONS GARLIC POWDER

5 TABLESPOONS DRIED LEMON PEEL OR
3 TABLESPOONS LEMON PEEL GRANULES

2 TEASPOONS SUGAR

1. Combine the peppercorns and coriander in a small skillet over medium-low heat. Cook for 2 to 3 minutes, stirring constantly until the coriander seeds start to split and the spices release a fragrant scent and become slightly darker. Transfer the spices to a plate and set aside to cool for 2 minutes.

2. Combine the toasted spices, salt, garlic powder, dried lemon peel, and sugar in a coffee or spice grinder. Pulse about 10 times (you do not want a fine powder), until the spices are coarsely ground. Transfer the ground spices to an airtight glass jar. Store in a cool, dry place away from sunlight. Use within 2 months.

Steak and Chop Rub

I like to combine several tablespoons of this tasty spice rub with Worcestershire or soy sauce and then use it to marinate steak or lamb chops before grilling. If there are leftovers, slice the meat thinly and serve over greens the next day. MAKES ABOUT ½ CUP

2 TABLESPOONS PAPRIKA	½ TEASPOON WHITE PEPPERCORNS
1 TABLESPOON GROUND TURMERIC	½ TEASPOON CARDAMOM SEEDS
2 TABLESPOONS FENNEL SEEDS	2 TABLESPOONS DRIED PARSLEY
1 ½ TABLESPOONS GARLIC SALT	1 TABLESPOON DRIED THYME
1 ½ TEASPOONS BLACK PEPPERCORNS	2 TEASPOONS SUGAR

Combine the paprika, turmeric, fennel seeds, garlic salt, black and white peppercorns, cardamom seeds, parsley, thyme, and sugar in a medium bowl and mix well. Transfer the spices to a coffee or spice grinder and pulse a few times, until coarsely ground. Transfer the ground spices to an airtight glass jar. Store in a cool, dry place away from sunlight. Use within 3 months.

Green Seafood Rub

I love the sweet aroma this spice rub adds to seafood dishes, especially shrimp, which stays sweet, soft, and juicy in the inside with a crispy herbed crust on the outside. It's also lovely on trout: Combine a few spoonfuls with olive oil, rub all over the fish, and then simply bake the fish. Kids love it for its mild flavor. Fragrant dried herbs like parsley, grayish green fennel, and thyme give this rub a natural green color. The cumin and lemon peel contain essential oils that balance the odor of seafood.

MAKES ABOUT ½ CUP

¼ CUP DRIED PARSLEY	½ TEASPOON GROUND FENNEL
3 TABLESPOONS DRIED LEMON PEEL	½ TEASPOON GROUND CUMIN
2 TABLESPOONS PAPRIKA	1 TABLESPOON DRIED THYME
1 ½ TABLESPOONS GARLIC SALT	2 TEASPOONS SUGAR

Combine the parsley, dried lemon peel, paprika, garlic salt, fennel, cumin, thyme, and sugar in a small bowl and mix well. Transfer the spices to a coffee or spice grinder and pulse a few times, until coarsely ground. Transfer the ground spices to an airtight glass jar. Store in a cool, dry place away from sunlight. Use within 3 months.

Spice Pastes Throughout Southeast Asia, the rhythm of the mortar and pestle pounding fresh aromatics can be heard coming from home kitchens. The refreshing aroma awakens the cook's senses. I like to refer to spice pastes as a cook's little helpers. Purple-red shallots, pungent garlic, fragrant kaffir lime leaves, galangal, lemongrass, luscious chiles, and earthy ginger are all fundamental ingredients that give depth to spice pastes. Salty and sour ingredients like salt, shrimp paste, fish sauce, tamarind juice, and even tomato are also added to draw out the flavor of the spices. Some Southeast Asian cooks prefer to use more fish sauce to make the dish saltier, while others may add more tamarind to accentuate the sourness. Finally, caramel-like palm sugar is added to many pastes, not for its sweetness, but rather to balance the flavors, creating a sweet, salty, sour, spicy, and bitter taste in the food. When you use a spice paste to begin your stir-fries, curries, soups, and stews, the majority of your flavors are already created. You only need to decide on your main ingredient.

Traditional Sambal Blending dried chiles for reddish color with onions and tomato for tart flavor is the starting point of this basic spice paste recipe. Use this as a base for stir-frying vegetables, meat, poultry, or seafood or serve it with grilled seafood. There are numerous ways to vary this sambal recipe. If you are in the mood for Thai, balance the paste with fish sauce, lime juice, and palm sugar. For Malaysian and Indonesian, add shrimp paste, coconut milk, palm sugar, and tamarind. For Vietnamese, add fish sauce, tamarind, garlic, and sugar. My students often tell me that this is the most inspiring paste. The fun lies in discovering how to tweak the ingredients. MAKES ABOUT 1½ CUPS

¼ CUP ROUGHLY BROKEN DRIED RED CHILES, OR TO TASTE

1 MEDIUM ONION, CHOPPED

3 MEDIUM TOMATOES, HALVED

¼ CUP VEGETABLE OIL

2½ TABLESPOONS SUGAR

1 TEASPOON SALT, OR TO TASTE

1 TABLESPOON SHRIMP PASTE, TOASTED (PAGE 34)

1. Soak the dried chiles in ¼ cup hot water for 15 minutes, until soft. Drain, reserving the soaking water.

2. Combine the chiles, onion, and tomatoes in a food processor. Blend until smooth, using some of the chile-soaking water to facilitate the blending. The paste should be light orange when well pureed.

3. Heat the oil in a large wok or sauté pan over medium heat. Carefully pour the blended paste into the wok and stir well. Reduce the heat to medium-low and cook for 30 minutes, until the paste appears deep orange. The paste is cooked when aromatic and the oils appear on the surface.

4. Season the paste with the sugar, salt, and shrimp paste. Stir well and raise the heat to high. Bring the paste to a boil and cook for 2 to 3 minutes, stirring occasionally to prevent the paste from burning. Remove from the heat and set aside to cool before using. Transfer the paste to an airtight container and store for up to 4 days in the refrigerator or 3 months in the freezer.

Merchant's
Curry
Powders,
Rubs,
Spice
Pastes,
and Sauces
55

Thai Red Curry Paste

The color of this paste comes from the liberal use of dried red chiles. Use this paste to make a vegetable, chicken, or duck curry or simply add it to your pan as a base for stir-frying or put a dash in your favorite marinade for the added zing. MAKES ABOUT ½ CUP

10 TO 15 DRIED RED CHILES, TO TASTE

½ TEASPOON CORIANDER SEEDS

2 TEASPOONS SALT

2 TEASPOONS FRESHLY GROUND WHITE PEPPER

ONE 3-INCH PIECE FRESH GALANGAL, SLICED

2 STALKS FRESH LEMONGRASS, BOTTOM PART ONLY, SLICED

8 FRESH KAFFIR LIME LEAVES, STEMMED AND TORN INTO SMALL PIECES

6 GARLIC CLOVES, CHOPPED

4 SMALL SHALLOTS, SLICED

1 TABLESPOON SHRIMP PASTE, TOASTED (PAGE 34)

1. Soak the dried chiles in ½ cup hot water for 10 to 15 minutes, until soft.

2. Put the coriander seeds in a small skillet over medium-low heat. Cook for a few seconds, until fragrant. Set aside on a plate to cool. Using a stone mortar and pestle or a coffee or spice grinder, finely grind the coriander. Set aside.

3. Remove the chiles from the water and squeeze them dry. Save the soaking water only if you are using a food processor to grind the spices.

4. To prepare the curry paste using a mortar and pestle, start with the chiles, salt, and pepper and pound until smooth. Next add the galangal and pound again. Then add the lemongrass, lime leaves, garlic, and shallots and pound again until pastelike. Finally, add the shrimp paste and the toasted ground coriander and mix well. Alternatively, put all the ingredients in a food processor and grind to a paste with a little of the reserved chile-soaking water to facilitate the blending. Transfer the paste to an airtight container and store for up to 1 week in the refrigerator or 3 months in the freezer.

Thai Green Curry Paste

It was 1989 when I first tasted green curry, in a small restaurant called Thai Jazzaraunt in Jalan Tun Razak, Kuala Lumpur. I was totally taken by the deliciously balanced flavors in every spoonful. The secret is in the selection of spices, carefully pounded to a paste in a mortar and pestle. If you like your dish spicy, add more chiles to this paste rather than piling them on the dish at the last minute. To this day, green curry is one of my favorites, and I use this paste not just for Thai curries but also in many stir-fried dishes. MAKES ABOUT ½ CUP

½ TEASPOON CORIANDER SEEDS

½ TEASPOON CUMIN SEEDS

½ TEASPOON BLACK PEPPERCORNS

2 STAR ANISE, BROKEN INTO SMALL PIECES

1 TEASPOON SALT

10 FRESH GREEN BIRD'S EYE CHILES

TWO 1-INCH PIECES FRESH GALANGAL, SLICED

2 STALKS FRESH LEMONGRASS, BOTTOM PART ONLY, SLICED

2 TABLESPOONS CHOPPED CILANTRO STEMS

½ CUP FRESH CILANTRO LEAVES, CHOPPED

8 FRESH KAFFIR LIME LEAVES, STEMMED AND TORN INTO SMALL PIECES

4 GARLIC CLOVES, CHOPPED

2 SMALL SHALLOTS, SLICED

2 TEASPOONS SHRIMP PASTE, TOASTED (PAGE 34; OPTIONAL)

1. Combine the coriander, cumin, peppercorns, and star anise in a small skillet over medium-low heat. Cook the spices for a few seconds, until fragrant. Set aside on a plate to cool.

2. Using a stone mortar and pestle or a coffee or spice grinder, finely grind the toasted spices.

3. To prepare the curry paste using a mortar and pestle, start with the salt and green chiles and pound to fine paste. Next add the galangal and pound again. Then add the lemongrass a little at a time and pound until smooth. Add the cilantro stems and leaves and pound again. Add the lime leaves, garlic, and shallots and pound to make a smooth paste. Finally add the shrimp paste if you are using it and the ground spices and mix well. Alternatively, put all the ingredients in a food processor and grind to a paste with a little water to facilitate the blending. Transfer the paste to an airtight container and store for up to 1 week in the refrigerator or 3 months in the freezer.

Merchant's
Curry
Powders,
Rubs,
Spice
Pastes,
and Sauces
57

Thai Massaman Curry Paste

Massaman curry was introduced at the time of King Phra Buddha (Rama I), who was the first king of the Chakkri Dynasty to establish Bangkok as the capital of Thailand. It originated when Indian Muslim traders introduced their dry spices to Thailand, where cooks started using them along with their home-grown fresh spices. The paste was initially used to prepare Massaman curry, which translates as "Indian Muslim curry." Traditionally, this curry paste is used for cooking red meats like beef or lamb, but I have altered the recipe to make it suitable for use with poultry and stir-fried vegetables as well.

MAKES ABOUT ½ CUP

TWO 1-INCH CINNAMON STICKS, CRUSHED	½ TEASPOON CUMIN SEEDS
4 STAR ANISE, BROKEN INTO SMALL PIECES	1 TEASPOON SALT
	2 TEASPOONS MINCED FRESH GALANGAL
½ TEASPOON BLACK PEPPERCORNS	4 STALKS FRESH LEMONGRASS, BOTTOM PART ONLY, SLICED
4 CLOVES	
6 GREEN CARDAMOM PODS, CRUSHED	8 GARLIC CLOVES, SLICED
6 MILD DRIED RED CHILES, SEEDED AND BROKEN INTO SMALL PIECES	8 SMALL SHALLOTS, FINELY SLICED

1. Combine the cinnamon, star anise, peppercorns, cloves, cardamom, and chiles in a small wok or sauté pan over medium-low heat. Cook for a few seconds, until the spices are fragrant and the chiles slightly blackened. Remove from the heat and set aside on a plate to cool. Next add the cumin and cook for 30 seconds, until fragrant. Remove from the heat and set aside to cool.

2. Using a mortar and pestle or a coffee or spice grinder, grind the toasted spices with the salt until fine. Remove and set aside.

3. To prepare the curry paste using a mortar and pestle, start with the galangal and pound until smooth. Next add the lemongrass and pound until smooth. Add the garlic and shallots and pound to a paste. Add the ground toasted spices and mix well. Alternatively, put all the ingredients in a food processor and grind to a paste with a little water to facilitate the blending. Transfer the paste to an airtight container and store for up to 1 week in the refrigerator or 3 months in the freezer.

Ginger-Garlic Paste

The Southeast Asian way of cooking involves taking spices and aromatics as a foundation and layering them with other ingredients. Starting your cooking with Ginger-Garlic Paste will result in a myriad of distinct flavors. Preparing this paste in advance is a terrific time-saver, because you won't have to peel and grind the garlic and ginger for each use. Refrigerate it or freeze it in small portions. Use only a few tablespoons of this paste to begin your curry dish. This paste is also a natural meat and poultry tenderizer. MAKES ABOUT 1 CUP

ONE 12-INCH PIECE FRESH GINGER, PEELED AND CHOPPED (ABOUT 1 CUP)

20 GARLIC CLOVES, PEELED (ABOUT ½ CUP)

Combine the ginger, the garlic, and 3 tablespoons water in a food processor. Blend into an aromatic paste, scraping down the sides every so often if needed. Transfer the paste to an airtight container and store for up to 1 week in the refrigerator or 3 months in the freezer.

Cilantro-Garlic Paste

My students often ask what makes my Thai curries and stir-fries subtle yet complex, with delicately perfumed and well-balanced flavors. The secret lies in Cilantro-Garlic Paste. I use this paste in everything from marinades to curries for its fresh kick. For this particular paste, the root of the cilantro plant—also known as *coriander root*—has the most concentrated flavor. Cilantro root can be found in the frozen section of Southeast Asian grocery stores. Use the cilantro stems if you can't find the roots.

MAKES ABOUT 1 CUP

½ CUP ROUGHLY CHOPPED CILANTRO ROOTS OR ½ CUP STEMS

30 GARLIC CLOVES, PEELED

2 TEASPOONS BLACK PEPPERCORNS

1 TEASPOON SALT

2 TABLESPOONS VEGETABLE OIL

1. Combine the cilantro, garlic, black peppercorns, and salt in a food processor and pulse until finely ground, about 40 seconds scraping down the sides every so often if needed.

2. With the machine running, slowly add the oil in a steady stream. After all the oil has been added, pulse to combine for 30 seconds. Transfer the paste to an airtight container and store for up to 1 week in the refrigerator or 3 months in the freezer.

Roasted Chile Paste This paste gets its bite from dried red chiles and shallots and its delicate sweetness from palm sugar and sweet soy sauce. Stir this paste into salad dressings and soups and as the final ingredient in stir-fries. If you do not have time to make your own, you can substitute store-bought chile paste in recipes that call for Roasted Chile Paste. Look for a deep reddish brown chile paste in oil in a glass jar that reads "Thai Chili Paste" or "Nam Prik Pao." The best brands are Pantainorasingh and Mae Pranom. MAKES ABOUT 1½ CUPS

½ CUP DRIED RED CHILES

4 SMALL SHALLOTS, PEELED AND CUT IN HALF

10 GARLIC CLOVES, PEELED

¼ CUP PLUS 2 TABLESPOONS VEGETABLE OIL

½ CUP PLUS 2 TABLESPOONS PALM SUGAR SYRUP (PAGE 27) OR BROWN SUGAR

2 TABLESPOONS SWEET SOY SAUCE

2 TEASPOONS SALT

½ CUP TAMARIND LIQUID (PAGE 35)

1 TEASPOON SHRIMP PASTE, TOASTED (PAGE 34)

1. Combine the chiles, shallots, and garlic in a heavy skillet over medium heat. Cook until the garlic cloves are golden brown, turning them frequently so they do not burn, about 10 minutes. Remove from the heat and set aside to cool.

2. Put the chiles, shallots, and garlic in a food processor and grind them until smooth. With the food processor running, slowly add half of the oil in a steady stream. Process the ingredients until pureed.

3. Heat the remaining 3 tablespoons oil in a wok or sauté pan over medium heat, add the blended chile paste, and cook, stirring frequently, until the oil appears on the top, about 15 minutes.

4. Add the palm sugar syrup, sweet soy sauce, salt, and tamarind liquid, reduce the heat to low, and cook for 3 minutes, until the paste is deep red. Add the shrimp paste and cook for 1 minute. At this point, the chile paste should appear thick, like jam, with a little oil on top. The paste should taste sweet, spicy, salty, and a little sour.

5. Remove from the heat and set aside to cool. Transfer the paste to an airtight container and store for up to 1 week in the refrigerator or 1 month in the freezer.

Cook's Tip *For vegetarians, substitute salt to taste for the shrimp paste.*

Merchant's
Curry
Powders,
Rubs,
Spice
Pastes,
and Sauces
61

Seafood Spice Paste Here spices are combined to accentuate the flavors of any type of seafood. Fresh red chiles and shallots add heat, while ginger, lemongrass, and coriander seeds enhance the aroma of the seafood. The nuts complement the seafood without overpowering its taste and texture. There are countless ways in which to use this aromatic paste: Sauté it at the beginning of your cooking and then add the seafood of your choice. Or blend the paste with coconut milk or broth to produce a sauce for simmering seafood. Brush it on seafood before grilling, mix it with seafood to make kebabs and satays, or use it as a base for stir-fries. The combined spices give this paste a beautiful orange color to make your meals a hit. MAKES ABOUT 2 CUPS

10 FRESH RED CHILES, CHOPPED

3 SMALL SHALLOTS, PEELED AND CUT IN HALF

5 GARLIC CLOVES, PEELED

ONE 3-INCH PIECE FRESH TURMERIC, SLICED, OR 1 TEASPOON GROUND TURMERIC

ONE 1-INCH PIECE FRESH GINGER, PEELED AND SLICED

10 CANDLENUTS OR MACADAMIA NUTS, CRUSHED

1 TOMATO, CUT IN HALF, SEEDED, AND SLICED

2 TEASPOONS SHRIMP PASTE, TOASTED (PAGE 34)

1 TEASPOON CORIANDER SEEDS, CRUSHED

2 TEASPOONS SALT, OR TO TASTE

⅓ CUP VEGETABLE OIL

4 STALKS FRESH LEMONGRASS, BOTTOM PART ONLY, BRUISED

1. Combine the chiles, shallots, garlic, turmeric, ginger, candlenuts, tomato, shrimp paste, coriander, and salt in a food processor and grind into a paste, using a little water if needed to facilitate the blending.

2. Heat the oil in a wok or sauté pan over medium heat. Carefully pour in the paste and add the lemongrass to the pan. Bring to a simmer, then reduce the heat to medium-low and simmer, stirring occasionally to prevent sticking, until all the water has evaporated, 25 to 30 minutes. The paste is cooked when the oils have separated on the surface and the paste is yellowish orange and fragrant.

3. Taste the spice paste for salt and tweak to your liking. Remove from the heat and set aside to cool before using. Transfer the paste to an airtight container and store for up to 1 week in the refrigerator or 3 months in the freezer.

Chicken Spice Paste

From Bali to Bangkok, I have always enjoyed chicken, whether slow-roasted over a charcoal fire or deep-fried indoors. This spice paste makes chicken even better, giving it a beautiful golden color from spices like turmeric and freshness from galangal, garlic, and lemongrass. The flavor of the paste comes alive when palm sugar syrup is added to balance the aromatic spices, giving it a mild caramel-like sweetness. I prepare a lot of this paste and freeze it to speed up my weeknight meals. Mix it with olive oil, then use it to baste chicken when baking or grilling, blend it with coconut milk to make a mellow chicken curry, or use it as a base paste for stir-fries. MAKES ABOUT 1½ CUPS

5 TO 10 FRESH RED BIRD'S-EYE CHILES OR 4 FRESH RED JALAPEÑO CHILES, CHOPPED, TO TASTE

3 SMALL SHALLOTS, PEELED AND CUT IN HALF

10 GARLIC CLOVES, PEELED

ONE 2-INCH PIECE FRESH TURMERIC, SLICED, OR ½ TEASPOON GROUND TURMERIC

ONE 2-INCH PIECE FRESH GALANGAL, SLICED

10 CANDLENUTS OR MACADAMIA NUTS, CRUSHED

⅓ CUP VEGETABLE OIL

4 STALKS FRESH LEMONGRASS, BOTTOM PART ONLY, BRUISED

½ CUP PALM SUGAR SYRUP (PAGE 27) OR BROWN SUGAR, OR TO TASTE

1 TEASPOON SALT, OR TO TASTE

1. Combine the chiles, shallots, garlic, turmeric, galangal, and candlenuts in a food processor and grind into a paste, using a little water if needed to facilitate the blending.

2. Heat the oil in a wok or sauté pan over medium heat. Carefully pour in the paste and add the lemongrass, palm sugar syrup, salt, and ⅓ cup water. Bring to a simmer, then reduce the heat to medium-low and simmer, stirring occasionally to prevent sticking, until all the water has evaporated, about 20 minutes. The paste is cooked when the oils have separated on the surface and the paste is golden brown and fragrant.

3. Taste and add sugar or salt if needed. Remove from the heat and set aside to cool before using. Transfer the paste to an airtight container and store for up to 1 week in the refrigerator or 3 months in the freezer.

Sauces and Marinades Soy, oyster, sweet soy, and fish sauces are indispensable to Southeast Asian cooking. Combined with other ingredients in the pantry, such as coconut milk, garam masala, honey, palm sugar, and aromatics, they produce a variety of flavors at once. Recipes in this section, such as Sweet-Sour Sauce and Perfect Peanut Sauce, can be tossed with meat, seafood, vegetables, or salads to make your family meals effortless.

Sweet-Sour Sauce

This sauce's natural sweetness comes from fresh pineapple and onions, its tartness from rice vinegar, its saltiness from fish sauce, and its spicy taste from chile, creating an indisputably Southeast Asian flavor. I find this delicious sauce extremely adaptable. Some days I use it to make quick sweet and sour pork or shrimp. On other days I drizzle it over poached or fried eggs or serve it with fresh vegetables or spring rolls. MAKES 2 CUPS

1½ CUPS PEELED, CORED, AND CHOPPED FRESH PINEAPPLE

½ MEDIUM WHITE ONION, CHOPPED

5 GARLIC CLOVES, PEELED

1 FRESH RED CHILE, SLICED

2 TEASPOONS RICE VINEGAR

⅓ CUP PLUS 3 TABLESPOONS SUGAR

½ CUP KETCHUP

1½ TABLESPOONS FISH SAUCE

½ TEASPOON SALT

1 Combine the pineapple, onion, garlic, chile, and vinegar in a food processor and grind to a paste.

2. Transfer the pineapple paste to a medium saucepan over medium heat. Add the sugar, ketchup, fish sauce, and salt and bring to a boil, stirring gently every so often. Cook until the sauce thickens, about 5 minutes.

3. Remove from the heat and let cool. Transfer to an airtight container and store for up to 1 week in the refrigerator or 1 month in the freezer.

Merchant's
Curry
Powders,
Rubs,
Spice
Pastes,
and Sauces
65

Perfect Peanut Sauce

For a large number of Southeast Asians, hunting down good peanut sauce is a serious pursuit. The best peanut sauce is, without doubt, made by the satayman, a street peddler who specializes in spiced meat threaded onto bamboo skewers and grilled over glowing charcoal. The satay peddler serves his specialty with the perfect peanut sauce, and he does not take shortcuts. You will not be disappointed making this sauce from scratch. The best sauce is yellowish orange, semisweet, and never gooey. The aroma of peanuts roasting in the oven and the fresh nutty taste that the sauce brings to any dish are irresistible. You can pour this sauce over salads or use it to make quick stir-fry chicken with peanut sauce. It's delicious. MAKES 4 CUPS

3 CUPS UNSALTED RAW PEANUTS (ABOUT 1 POUND)

7 GARLIC CLOVES, PEELED

6 FRESH RED BIRD'S-EYE CHILES OR 4 FRESH RED JALAPEÑO CHILES, CHOPPED

ONE 3-INCH PIECE FRESH GALANGAL, SLICED

ONE 3-INCH PIECE FRESH TURMERIC, CHOPPED, OR ½ TEASPOON GROUND TURMERIC

2 CUPS CANNED COCONUT MILK (PAGE 26)

¼ TEASPOON GROUND CORIANDER

¼ TEASPOON GROUND CUMIN

4 FRESH KAFFIR LIME LEAVES, STEMMED AND TORN

3 TABLESPOONS PALM SUGAR SYRUP (PAGE 27) OR BROWN SUGAR

¼ CUP SWEET SOY SAUCE

JUICE OF 1 LIME

½ TEASPOON SALT, OR TO TASTE

1. Preheat the oven to 350°F.

2. Spread the peanuts on a baking sheet and roast in the oven for 15 minutes, or until golden brown. Immediately transfer the peanuts to a plate to cool.

3. Put the peanuts in a food processor and blend for about 20 seconds, or until finely ground. Add the garlic, chiles, galangal, and turmeric to the food processor and grind until smooth, adding a little water if needed to facilitate the blending.

4. Put the paste into a heavy pot or Dutch oven and add the coconut milk, 2 cups water, the coriander, cumin, and lime leaves. Bring to a boil, then lower the heat and simmer for 10 minutes, stirring frequently to prevent the coconut milk from burning and sticking.

5. Add the palm sugar syrup, sweet soy sauce, lime juice, and salt to the pot. When you add the sweet soy sauce, the sauce will turn the color of a roasted peanut. Bring just to a boil, lower the heat, and simmer for 5 minutes, stirring periodically, until a little oil has separated and appears on the surface. Serve hot or cool. Transfer to an airtight container and store for up to 4 days in the refrigerator or 1 month in the freezer.

*Merchant's
Curry
Powders,
Rubs,
Spice
Pastes,
and Sauces*
67

Merchant's Barbecue Sauce

Every time I prepare this sauce in my Seattle kitchen, I remember the Chinese sauce man and the loud hoot from his van. He maneuvered the tiny back roads of Bangsar, a suburb of Kuala Lumpur, and often parked on the wrong side of the street. For years my family purchased a variety of sauces from him. In the kitchen, my mom would say "the vendor's sauce combined with a spoonful of Steak and Chop Rub [page 52] and a good cut of meat is all you need." After that, there's only one decision to make: should we grill or panfry the meat? MAKES 1½ CUPS

⅓ CUP SOY SAUCE

¼ CUP OYSTER SAUCE

2 TABLESPOONS SWEET SOY SAUCE

⅓ CUP KETCHUP

½ CUP HONEY

2 TEASPOONS GARAM MASALA (PAGE 46 OR STORE-BOUGHT)

1 TEASPOON GROUND MUSTARD

Combine the soy sauce, oyster sauce, sweet soy sauce, ketchup, honey, garam masala, and ground mustard in a bowl and whisk to mix well. Transfer to an airtight container and store for up to 1 week in the refrigerator or 1 month in the freezer.

Appetizers

Lemon Pepper Wings

✦

Miniature Spring Rolls

✦

Coconut Spareribs

✦

Sweet and Sour Meatballs Wrapped in Lettuce

✦

Golden Curry Puffs

✦

Spinach-Wrapped Savories

✦

Chicken Satay

✦

Lamb Satay

✦

Fragrant Seafood Cakes

No matter how busy the day, when I was young my family would always get together on the veranda for afternoon tea and homemade snacks, a Southeast Asian tradition akin to cocktails and hors d'oeuvres, to hold us over until dinner. My mother, my aunt, and I would scurry off to the kitchen in the late afternoon to whip something up.

I would pull out a can of sardines from the cupboard, mashing it with chopped shallots, chiles, tomatoes, ground fennel, fresh lemon juice, and herbs from our garden to make a spread for sandwiches. My aunt would busy herself preparing another treat, often repurposing leftovers such as minced beef and curried potatoes into little bites for tea. Sometimes extras, like lentil patties or banana fritters that my father had purchased on the way home from a roadside stand, became welcome additions to what we had prepared at home. My mother would scoop tea leaves from one of her many miniature canisters, and within minutes her fragrant brew of Ceylon tea would be placed graciously on the table, sometimes with a few cloves and a cinnamon stick added to the pot.

By five, the gathering would have reached its peak, with unexpected guests and energetic kids recounting their tales of the day. Just as we warmed to the stories, the distinct sound of a food peddler knocking an empty glass with a spoon would jolt us to run in his direction with empty bowls in our hands. He sold charcoal-grilled tofu filled with sliced cucumber and blanched bean sprouts laced with a thick peanut sauce; we could never quite replicate his generations-old recipe at home.

In Kuala Lumpur, snacks are often sold on the street by peddlers who set up makeshift stalls at sundown in residential neighborhoods. Their tarpaulin shades in a riot of colors strike a nostalgic, funfair atmosphere against the warm hues of the setting sun. Each peddler offers a signature dish, from spring rolls or grilled chicken wings to *mee goreng,* a stir-fried vermicelli dish with an assortment of vegetables.

Most peddlers are named after the food they sell. For example, no night market is complete without the dip-dip man, who sells bite-size pieces of fish, squid, octopus, crab balls, tofu, and more on bamboo skewers neatly arranged on baking trays. After his customers have made their selection, they dip their skewers in boiling broth to cook them and then savor them with either sweet chile or hoisin sauce. Customers are later billed according to the number of empty skewers.

My favorite snack is the ever popular *roti chanai*, a hot griddle bread made from wheat flour. There is artistry in tossing the dough akin to that of making pizza. The dough is kneaded with a little oil on a marble slab and thinned to obtain the round shape. The roti man then tosses the dough in the air to further stretch it to form layers. Once grilled, the roti chanai is flaky and soft with every bite. It is best dipped in creamy lentil or fish curry and enjoyed with a hot cup of spice tea.

The recipes in this chapter, many of my favorite street snacks, are perfect for sharing with family and friends. For a warm afternoon gathering, try Lemon Pepper Wings, Golden Curry Puffs, or Chicken Satay. For a late-night snack, nothing satisfies like Sweet and Sour Meatballs Wrapped in Lettuce. All of these dishes are quick and delicious—the perfect bite for any occasion.

Lemon Pepper Wings

When I prepare these wings, I reminisce about picnics, an old Peugeot, and Port Dickson. Growing up in an urban environment, my *apah* (dad) always wanted us to take in the sights and sounds of rural picturesque Port Dickson, a breezy seaside village just two hours from Kuala Lumpur. Packed in his old Peugeot for the two-hour trip, we would bubble with anticipation because my *amma* (mother) never failed to bring along a picnic basket filled with lemon pepper chicken wings. Of course, we spiced up the trip with stops at cliffs along the way, where we looked down on the rushing emerald waters of Port Dickson. Once we were out of the car, out came the picnic basket filled with the tasty wings, lots of pita bread, and mango chutney.

In this exceptional dish, Lemon Pepper Rub and yogurt give chicken wings incredible flavor and tenderness, making them an all-time favorite with adults and children alike. Feel free to substitute either chicken breast or thigh meat. If you do, cut the meat into cubes and serve on toothpicks. When I make this at home for my family, I normally serve the chicken on romaine lettuce topped with Pineapple Pickle (page 197), which also makes for a very satisfying lunch.

MAKES ABOUT 35 WINGS

2½ POUNDS CHICKEN WINGS	½ TEASPOON GARAM MASALA (PAGE 46 OR STORE-BOUGHT)
JUICE OF 1 LEMON	
2 TEASPOONS PAPRIKA	3 TABLESPOONS LEMON PEPPER RUB (PAGE 51)
1 TEASPOON SALT	
1¾ CUPS YOGURT	LEMON OR LIME WEDGES FOR GARNISH
3 TABLESPOONS GINGER-GARLIC PASTE (PAGE 59)	

1. Cut the wings in half at the joint. Discard the wing tips (the smaller section of the wings). Make 2 deep cuts in the skin side of each chicken wing, deep enough to touch the bone. Put the chicken wings in a large bowl.

2. Mix together the lemon juice, paprika, and salt. Rub each chicken piece thoroughly with the mixture. Cover and refrigerate for 30 minutes. The marinade will tenderize the chicken and give it a lovely color afterward.

3. Combine the yogurt, ginger-garlic paste, garam masala, and lemon pepper rub in a medium bowl. Whisk until smooth. Pour the marinade over the chicken and mix thoroughly with your hands, making sure the marinade gets into the cuts on the chicken pieces. Cover the bowl with plastic wrap and marinate the chicken in the refrigerator for at least 6 hours, preferably overnight. The golden rule with most meats is that the longer the meat marinates, the better it will taste.

4. Preheat the oven to 350°F. Remove the wings from the marinade and arrange on an oiled rack. Place the rack on a baking pan. Bake for 15 minutes, brushing with the remaining marinade periodically.

5. Turn the oven up to broil, and cook the wings until browned and crisp on the outside and tender on the inside, 5 to 7 minutes on each side. Serve hot or at room temperature, garnished with the lemon or lime wedges.

Miniature Spring Rolls

These crispy rolls, filled with minced shrimp, pork, and water chestnuts, are easy to prepare and are destined to become a family favorite. They are so good you may want to double the recipe. The rolls can be assembled ahead of time and kept in the refrigerator or freezer until you are ready to cook, making them ideal for entertaining. Plus they are small enough to pop into your mouth in a single bite. MAKES 25 MINI SPRING ROLLS

Dipping Sauce
½ CUP SUGAR

½ CUP RICE VINEGAR

1 TEASPOON MINCED GARLIC

5 FRESH RED CHILES, MINCED

¼ CUP FISH SAUCE

JUICE OF ½ ORANGE

Spring Rolls
8 OUNCES LARGE SHRIMP, PEELED AND DEVEINED

8 OUNCES GROUND PORK

ONE 5-OUNCE CAN WHOLE PEELED WATER CHESTNUTS, DRAINED AND CHOPPED

6 SHIITAKE MUSHROOM CAPS, SLICED

3 SCALLIONS, BOTH WHITE AND GREEN PARTS, CHOPPED

3 GARLIC CLOVES, PEELED

2 TABLESPOONS SWEET SOY SAUCE

2 TABLESPOONS FISH SAUCE

1 TEASPOON SUGAR

ONE 16-OUNCE PACKAGE 5-INCH-SQUARE SPRING ROLL WRAPPERS

1 LARGE EGG, LIGHTLY BEATEN WITH 1 TEASPOON WATER

VEGETABLE OR PEANUT OIL FOR FRYING

1. To make the dipping sauce, bring ¼ cup water to a boil in a saucepan. Add the sugar and vinegar and stir well to dissolve. Add the garlic and red chiles and bring to a boil. Add the fish sauce and orange juice and simmer over low heat until the sauce thickens, about 15 minutes. Remove from the heat and set aside to cool. The sauce can be refrigerated for up to 6 hours.

2. To make the filling, combine the shrimp, pork, water chestnuts, mushrooms, scallions, and garlic in a food processor. Pulse a few times until the ingredients are well combined but not mashed. Transfer to a bowl. Stir in the sweet soy sauce, fish sauce, and sugar and mix well to blend the flavors.

3. Lay 1 spring roll wrapper on a cutting board or clean surface. Put about 1 teaspoon of the filling in the center of the wrapper, about 1 inch from the edge closest to you. With a pastry brush, lightly brush the sides of the wrapper with the beaten egg to keep the spring rolls sealed during cooking. Fold the wrapper from the end closest to you to just cover the filling. Fold the sides of the wrapper toward the center. Using your fingers to gently squeeze the wrappers to make sure no air is trapped within, start to roll firmly into a cigar shape. Place the spring roll on a plate. Repeat with the remaining wrappers and filling. The uncooked rolls can be stored in an airtight bag in the freezer for up to 1 month. Do not thaw the spring rolls before frying.

4. Heat 2 to 3 inches of oil in a wok or large heavy pot over medium heat. Place a chopstick into the wok or pot: if the oil starts to bubble around the chopstick, the oil is ready for frying. Add a few spring rolls one at a time. Do not overcrowd the wok or pot or the spring rolls will become soggy. Fry, turning occasionally, until the spring rolls are golden and crisp, 5 to 7 minutes. Remove and drain on paper towels. Repeat until all the rolls are fried. Serve hot with dipping sauce.

Coconut Spareribs These succulent pork ribs are a hit in all my cooking classes and at my parties at home. The ribs are marinated in ginger, garlic, cilantro stems, and lemongrass, adding a sweet aroma and helping make the meat tender. I add coconut milk to give the ribs a smooth balance and an exotic taste. These ribs are also great done on the grill. SERVES 4

ONE 2-INCH PIECE FRESH GINGER, PEELED AND COARSELY CHOPPED

5 GARLIC CLOVES, PEELED

2 STALKS FRESH LEMONGRASS, BOTTOM PART ONLY, THINLY SLICED

¼ CUP CHOPPED CILANTRO STEMS

1 TEASPOON GARAM MASALA (PAGE 46 OR STORE-BOUGHT)

1 CUP HONEY

½ CUP CANNED COCONUT MILK (PAGE 26)

¼ CUP SWEET SOY SAUCE

¼ CUP SOY SAUCE

2 POUNDS PORK SPARERIBS

1. Combine the ginger, garlic, lemongrass, cilantro stems, garam masala, honey, coconut milk, sweet soy sauce, and soy sauce in a food processor. Blend the ingredients until smooth.

2. Place the spareribs in a glass baking dish. Rub the sauce over the spareribs with your hands. Cover and refrigerate the spareribs overnight.

3. When you are ready to cook the ribs, preheat the oven to 375°F. Place the ribs on a baking sheet lined with foil. Save the marinade for basting. Bake the ribs for 30 minutes, basting every 10 minutes.

4. Increase the oven temperature to 400°F and continue baking for 20 minutes, basting for the first 10 minutes only.

5. Turn the oven up to broil, and cook the ribs for 3 minutes, or until the meat is browned. Carefully remove the ribs from the oven and set them aside to cool before slicing into individual ribs and serving.

Sweet and Sour Meatballs Wrapped in Lettuce

This recipe reminds me of the time I waited in a long line in front of a crowded stall at Chatuchak Weekend Market in Bangkok. After a tiring walk hunting for souvenirs under the blazing sun, I needed to recharge. These meatballs on skewers, hot and sizzling with bursts of garlic and cilantro, were too hard to resist. The meatballs are simply divine when dipped in a sweet and sour sauce. MAKES 18 MEATBALLS

12 OUNCES GROUND PORK	VEGETABLE OIL FOR FRYING
2 TABLESPOONS CILANTRO-GARLIC PASTE (PAGE 60)	1 SMALL HEAD BOSTON OR BIBB LETTUCE, SEPARATED INTO LEAVES
½ TEASPOON SALT	1 CUP FRESH CILANTRO LEAVES
½ TEASPOON FRESHLY GROUND WHITE PEPPER	1 ½ CUPS SWEET-SOUR SAUCE (PAGE 65)
1 ½ TABLESPOONS FISH SAUCE	

1. Combine the pork, cilantro-garlic paste, salt, pepper, and fish sauce in a medium bowl. Mix well with your hands to blend the flavors.

2. With oiled hands to prevent sticking, form the mixture into balls about 1 inch in diameter by rolling it between your hands. Set the meatballs aside on a plate.

3. Heat 3 inches of oil in a wok or large heavy pot over medium heat. Place a chopstick into the wok or pot: if the oil starts to bubble around the chopstick, the oil is ready for frying. Add the meatballs one at a time. Do not overcrowd the wok or pot or the meatballs will break. Fry, turning occasionally, until the meatballs are golden, 5 to 7 minutes. Remove and drain on paper towels. Repeat until all the meatballs are fried.

4. To serve, arrange the lettuce leaves and cilantro on a platter. Pour the sweet-sour sauce into a small bowl and place on the platter. Spoon the meatballs next to the lettuce and cilantro and serve, encouraging guests to wrap them with cilantro in lettuce leaves before dipping into the sauce.

Cook's Tip *It's best to use ground pork with a fat content of at least 10 percent for this dish. The fat will provide flavor and prevent the meatballs from drying out.*

Golden Curry Puffs

Curry puffs are very popular teatime snacks in Malaysia. Prepared like Indian samosas, golden curry puffs are lightly spiced, drawing flavors from sweet potato, potato, and chicken. Typically, the pastry is homemade with flour, water, and butter and used to enclose the meat and veggie fillings. For this recipe I have chosen to use frozen puff pastry, available at most supermarkets, for convenience. MAKES ABOUT 22 PUFFS

1 CUP FROZEN PETITE PEAS

1 POUND FROZEN PUFF PASTRY

1 CARROT, DICED

1 MEDIUM SWEET POTATO, PEELED AND DICED

1 SMALL RED OR YUKON GOLD POTATO, PEELED AND DICED

2 TABLESPOONS VEGETABLE OIL

2 SPRIGS FRESH CURRY LEAVES, FINELY CHOPPED

ONE 2-INCH PIECE FRESH GINGER, PEELED AND MINCED

2 GARLIC CLOVES, CHOPPED

8 OUNCES BONELESS, SKINLESS CHICKEN BREAST, DICED

2 TABLESPOONS CURRY POWDER (PAGE 44 OR 45 OR STORE-BOUGHT)

1 TABLESPOON SUGAR

2 TEASPOONS SALT, OR TO TASTE

1 LARGE EGG, LIGHTLY BEATEN WITH 1 TEASPOON WATER

1. Preheat the oven to 400°F. Thaw the peas in a medium bowl filled with warm water for 10 minutes. Remove the puff pastry from the freezer and set aside to thaw.

2. Meanwhile, set up a steamer by bringing a couple of inches of water to a boil in a large pot. Place the carrot, sweet potato, potato, and peas in the steamer insert and set the insert over the boiling water. Cover and steam for 10 minutes, until the vegetables are tender. Set aside.

3. Heat the oil in a medium skillet over medium heat. When the oil is hot, add the curry leaves, ginger, and garlic and fry until the garlic is golden and the spices release a fragrant scent, 1 to 2 minutes. Add the chicken and curry powder and cook, stirring, until the meat is no longer pink, about 7 minutes.

4. Add the steamed vegetables, season with the sugar and salt, and cook for 3 to 4 minutes, until the ingredients are well combined. Remove from the heat and let cool completely.

5. When you are ready to make the curry puffs, lay one pastry sheet on a lightly floured surface. Roll out the dough until 1 inch wider all around. Cut the puff pastry sheet into 3-inch circles. Repeat with the remaining pastry. You will need about 22 circles.

6. Lightly brush the edges of the dough with the beaten egg. Place 1 tablespoon of the cooled filling in the center of each circle and then fold over the dough to form a semicircle. Gently seal the edges with a fork and place the curry puffs on a baking sheet. Brush each pastry with the beaten egg and bake until golden brown, about 25 minutes. Serve warm.

Spinach-Wrapped Savories

In Thailand, this healthy snack is called *miang kam*, but my cooking-class students like to call it "a party in your mouth." You can customize the flavors according to your taste, making this appetizer spicy, sweet, sour, or salty. If you decide to use the optional dried shrimp, you can find it in plastic packets or jars at any Asian grocery. These small, sun-dried shrimp are a deep salmon pink and firm to the touch. They add a unique salty flavor to the wraps. Since galangal is a tough rhizome, add a little water to your mini-chopper to facilitate the blending. When you serve this dish, your guests will be amazed at the combustion of flavors with each bite they take.

SERVES 6

---

1 CUP UNSWEETENED SHREDDED COCONUT

¾ CUP UNSALTED RAW PEANUTS

½ CUP DRIED SHRIMP (OPTIONAL)

ONE 3-INCH PIECE FRESH GALANGAL, SLICED

¼ CUP PALM SUGAR SYRUP (PAGE 27) OR BROWN SUGAR

2 TABLESPOONS FISH SAUCE

1 POUND FRESH SPINACH LEAVES

ONE 3-INCH PIECE FRESH GINGER, PEELED AND CUT INTO PEA-SIZED PIECES

4 SMALL SHALLOTS, DICED

1 LIME, CUT INTO SMALL WEDGES

3 FRESH GREEN OR RED BIRD'S-EYE CHILES, FINELY CHOPPED

---

1. Preheat the oven to 350°F. Put ½ cup of the coconut and ¼ cup of the peanuts on 2 separate baking sheets. Place the pan filled with peanuts on the bottom oven rack and the pan with the coconut on the top rack for even browning. Bake the coconut until golden brown, about 7 minutes. Stir the peanuts and leave them in the oven for 7 minutes longer, until golden. Let cool.

2. To make the coconut sauce, place the browned coconut and peanuts, ¼ cup of the dried shrimp if you are using it, and the galangal into a mini-chopper. Blend the ingredients into a coarse paste.

3. Combine the paste and 2 cups water in a saucepan over medium heat. Bring to a low boil, stirring every so often to prevent the paste from burning. Cook for 5 minutes, reduce the heat to low, and simmer the paste, stirring occasionally, until it thickens, 7 minutes.

4. Add the palm sugar syrup and fish sauce and continue to cook, stirring frequently, for 5 minutes, until the sauce caramelizes. The sauce should be glossy and thick with the consistency of jam. Remove from the heat and allow the sauce to cool.

5. Pour the sauce into a small bowl and place the bowl in the middle of a platter. Place the spinach leaves, the remaining roasted peanuts, coconut, and shrimp, the ginger, shallots, lime wedges, and chiles around the sauce. Encourage your guests to place a small amount of each ingredient on a spinach leaf, top with a spoonful of sauce, fold it up, and pop it into their mouths.

Chicken Satay The Turks have kebabs, the Greeks have souvlaki, and the Japanese have yakitori. In Southeast Asia we have satay: thin marinated strips of meat on bamboo skewers, cooked over a grill. Chicken or beef is the preferred meat. For an authentic and delicious flavor, grilling the satay over charcoal is best, but it also tastes good when cooked on the stovetop. Watching a satay chef at work is truly enjoyable. Standing over the hot grill, he holds a palm leaf in one hand to fan the fire and with the other skillfully turns over several skewers at a time to ensure that each cooks evenly. Serve these skewers of juicy meat piping hot with cubed or sliced cucumber, sliced onion, and Perfect Peanut Sauce (page 66).

MAKES ABOUT 20 SKEWERS

....

1½ POUNDS BONELESS, SKINLESS CHICKEN THIGHS, SLICED INTO 3-INCH STRIPS

5 FRESH RED OR GREEN BIRD'S-EYE CHILES, CHOPPED

¼ CUP PALM SUGAR SYRUP (PAGE 27) OR BROWN SUGAR

1 TEASPOON SALT

½ CUP CHICKEN SPICE PASTE (PAGE 63)

BAMBOO SKEWERS SOAKED IN WATER FOR 30 MINUTES

¼ CUP VEGETABLE OIL

....

1. Combine the chicken, chiles, palm sugar syrup, salt, and chicken spice paste in a bowl. Knead the meat and spices thoroughly to provide flavor and keep the meat moist and tender. Cover with plastic wrap and refrigerate for at least 4 hours or overnight.

2. Heat a grill to high. Thread the meat tightly onto the bamboo skewers. Place the skewers on the hot grill and cook, brushing periodically with the oil and turning frequently to keep the meat moist, until they are cooked through, 7 to 10 minutes. Alternatively, heat a nonstick grill pan over medium-high and cook the skewers, turning them and brushing them periodically with the oil, until they are evenly browned, about 10 minutes. Serve hot.

Lamb Satay In Bali, this satay is made using goat meat, but because I am absolutely wild about the taste of lamb, I use it in this recipe instead. Lamb is a full-flavored meat, so I suggest you use lots of freshly squeezed lime to accompany this dish. The lime accentuates the sweetness of the marinated meat.

MAKES ABOUT 30 SKEWERS

2 POUNDS BONELESS LAMB SHOULDER, CUT INTO ½-INCH CUBES

½ CUP SWEET SOY SAUCE

1 TEASPOON CORIANDER SEEDS, CRUSHED

½ TEASPOON BLACK PEPPERCORNS, CRUSHED

¼ TEASPOON WHITE PEPPERCORNS, CRUSHED

½ TEASPOON CUMIN SEEDS, CRUSHED

3 TABLESPOONS FRESH LIME JUICE

1 TEASPOON SALT

BAMBOO SKEWERS SOAKED IN WATER FOR 30 MINUTES

¼ CUP VEGETABLE OIL

4 LIMES, QUARTERED

1. Combine the lamb, sweet soy sauce, coriander, black and white pepper, cumin, lime juice, and salt in a bowl. Knead the meat and spices thoroughly to provide flavor and keep the meat moist and tender. Cover with plastic wrap and refrigerate for at least 4 hours or overnight.

2. Heat a grill to high. Thread the meat tightly onto the bamboo skewers. Place the skewers on the hot grill and cook, brushing periodically with the oil and turning frequently to keep the meat moist, until medium-well to well done, 12 to 15 minutes. Serve hot with lime wedges.

Fragrant Seafood Cakes

The delicate texture of seafood is enhanced with coconut and kaffir lime leaves, giving these cakes the most incredible fragrance. This recipe is perhaps the tastiest seafood cake you'll ever make. I love when the palm sugar caramelizes around the cakes during the cooking and the aroma fills the kitchen. These light cakes are best accompanied by Shallot and Lemongrass Sambal (page 200). MAKES 15 CAKES

1 POUND BONELESS, SKINLESS SNAPPER OR MAHIMAHI

8 OUNCES LARGE SHRIMP, PEELED AND DEVEINED

1 CUP FRESH OR THAWED FROZEN GRATED COCONUT

6 FRESH KAFFIR LIME LEAVES, STEMMED AND CHOPPED

1 TEASPOON SALT

1½ TEASPOONS WHITE PEPPERCORNS, CRUSHED

2 TABLESPOONS PALM SUGAR SYRUP (PAGE 27) OR BROWN SUGAR

½ CUP SEAFOOD SPICE PASTE (PAGE 62)

1. Preheat the oven to 375°F. Put the fish and shrimp into a food processor and pulse until you have a smooth paste. Add the coconut, lime leaves, salt, pepper, palm sugar syrup, and spice paste and pulse several times to mix well. Transfer the mixture to a bowl.

2. To make the seafood cakes, oil your hands, then take about 3 heaping tablespoons of the mixture, shape it into a ball, and then flatten the ball into a disk about 1 inch thick. Repeat with the remaining mixture. Place the cakes on a baking sheet and bake until golden, 15 to 20 minutes. Serve hot.

Salads and Soups

Vegetable and Tofu Salad with Peanut Sauce

✦

Papaya and Prawn Salad

✦

Peppered Beef Salad

✦

Green Apple and Mango Salad

✦

Balinese Tuna Salad

✦

Green Papaya Salad

✦

Spicy Seafood Salad

✦

Apple and Radish Raita

✦

**Pineapple, Jicama, and Green Mango
with Tamarind Sauce**

✦

Fragrant Coconut Milk and Seafood Soup

✦

Split Yellow Lentil Soup

✦

Hot and Sour Prawn Soup

It was a warm summer day in June. The air was dry and still in Washington, with the birds perched on my wooden fence breaking into melodious song. The roses were in full bloom, painting my walkway in shades of lilac, scarlet, red, and peach that accentuated the greens of my garden: cilantro, mint, basil, scallion, rosemary, chile peppers, and thyme.

I draped a Javanese sarong across my patio table and placed on top trays of freshly picked herbs and colorful bottles of seasoning sauces in preparation for a class I would be teaching on the salads and soups of Southeast Asia. While waiting for my students to arrive, I was taken back to a trip I made to Kelantan, the northeastern state of peninsular Malaysia, when I was in my early twenties.

Kelantan, often referred to as the "cradle of Malay culinary culture," emanates the Old World charm of quaint fishing villages, lush rice fields, and traditional pastimes. Sharing a border with Thailand, it draws together numerous culinary influences that give the food from this region a unique character. It is also the home of the Central Market of Kota Bharu, the state capital.

Winding through the busy narrow streets, I grew pleasantly aware of the pulse of this old city energetically coming to life. I passed coffee shops crowded with village folks rising early for their morning cup of *kopi o,* the locally brewed black coffee. Little roadside food stalls did brisk business selling hot homemade cakes to eager customers, and there was a long line for the not-to-be missed Kelantan *nasi kerabu,* a warm plate of coconut rice served with fresh herbs.

I finally arrived at the Central Market the locals call *pasar siti khatijah*. Making my way through its huge entrance, I could already smell what was inside: rows and rows of herbs and vegetables in a thousand shades of green. I was surprised to see children sitting beside their mother as she sold the herbs to busy housewives. Watching the children nibble on leaves of basil, mint, and cilantro proved to me that kids can be educated on the different flavors of herbs at an early age.

In Malaysia, a variety of these aromatic herbs, young shoots, leaves, flowers, fruits, and rhizomes are eaten as salads called *ulam*. In making ulam, herbs like mint, basil, cilantro, kaffir lime, turmeric leaves, papaya flowers, and young ginger shoots are finely sliced, then combined with coconut milk, pounded chiles, dried prawns, salted fish, roasted grated coconut, and fried shallots. This layering of ingredients creates texture and is a delicious way to make the most of fresh herbs.

In this chapter you'll find plenty of salads and soups inspired by ulams and the other dishes created from the hundreds of fresh herbs sold at the Central Market. Serve these dishes as full meals on a hot afternoon or as a delicious first course in any feast.

Vegetable and Tofu Salad with Peanut Sauce

The Indonesian island of Java is the birthplace of this fabulously healthy salad. At noon the street stalls, called *warung,* crowd with hungry patrons who gather there to relax, enjoy the passing street scene, and indulge in plates of crisp vegetables topped with spiced peanut sauce. This dish makes an excellent lunch, especially for vegetarians. The healthy vegetables like green beans and jícama are powerful antioxidants and contain folic acid and vitamins A and C. And remember, the sauce is what makes this healthy dish delicious. SERVES 4

4 OUNCES BEAN SPROUTS

12 OUNCES GREEN BEANS, TRIMMED AND CUT INTO 1-INCH PIECES

ONE 14-OUNCE PACKAGE FIRM TOFU, DRAINED AND CUT INTO 1-INCH CUBES

3 MEDIUM RED POTATOES, PEELED AND CUT INTO 1-INCH CUBES

1 MEDIUM ENGLISH CUCUMBER, CUT INTO 1-INCH CUBES

1 SMALL JÍCAMA, PEELED AND DICED

3 CUPS PERFECT PEANUT SAUCE (PAGE 66)

1. Half-fill a large stockpot with water and bring to a boil. Add the bean sprouts and boil for 10 seconds. Remove the sprouts from the water with a slotted spoon and immediately rinse under cold running water. Drain well and set aside on a plate. Add the green beans to the boiling water and cook for 30 seconds. Remove the green beans, drain, and cool. Place the tofu in the water and cook for 1 minute, until soft. Remove and set aside. Add the potatoes to the boiling water and cook for 10 minutes, or until tender. Drain and set aside to cool.

2. Arrange the bean sprouts, green beans, tofu, potatoes, cucumber, and jícama on individual plates, pour the peanut sauce over the vegetables, and serve.

Cook's Tip *Tempeh and spinach, broccoli, cabbage, watercress, and cauliflower florets are all excellent substitutes for tofu and the vegetables called for in this recipe.*

Papaya and Prawn Salad This salad is a favorite among my friends and students, who love how its beautifully balanced burst of sweet, sour, salty, and spicy flavors awakens their taste buds. A ripe Caribbean or Hawaiian papaya works best for this dish. Whichever you choose, prepare for absolute silence after the first forkful! SERVES 4

1 TABLESPOON FISH SAUCE

JUICE OF 2 LIMES

1 ½ TABLESPOONS SUGAR

3 SMALL SHALLOTS, THINLY SLICED

2 FRESH RED CHILES, THINLY SLICED

10 OUNCES MEDIUM PRAWNS OR LARGE SHRIMP, PEELED AND DEVEINED

½ TEASPOON SALT

1 TABLESPOON VEGETABLE OIL

1 RIPE MEDIUM PAPAYA, PEELED, SEEDED, AND DICED

1 RIPE MEDIUM MANGO, PEELED, PITTED, AND DICED

1 CUP FRESH MINT LEAVES, COARSELY CHOPPED

1 CUP FRESH CILANTRO LEAVES, COARSELY CHOPPED

2 TABLESPOONS UNSALTED ROASTED PEANUTS, ROUGHLY CHOPPED (OPTIONAL)

1. Preheat the broiler. To prepare the sauce, combine the fish sauce, lime juice, sugar, shallots, and chiles in a small bowl. Whisk until the sugar dissolves. Allow the seasoning sauce to sit for 5 minutes for the flavors to infuse.

2. Mix the prawns, salt, and oil in a medium bowl. Arrange the prawns on a baking sheet and place on the top rack underneath the broiler until the prawns turn bright pinkish orange and shrink slightly, about 3 minutes. Remove the prawns from the oven. Let cool for 1 minute.

3. To serve the salad, combine the papaya, mango, mint, cilantro, sauce, and prawns with any juice from the baking sheet and toss in a serving bowl. Garnish with chopped peanuts if desired.

Peppered Beef Salad This wonderful salad is a complete and healthy meal in itself. The steak is broiled for intense flavor and then mixed with a flavorful citrus dressing. The juicy steak, sliced cucumber, tomatoes, grapes, scallions, and herbs are loaded with essential vitamins, antioxidants, and minerals. The contrasting textures and colors also make this salad a visual feast. SERVES 4

⅔ CUP FRESH LIME JUICE

¼ CUP FISH SAUCE

¼ CUP PALM SUGAR SYRUP (PAGE 27) OR BROWN SUGAR

3 SERRANO CHILES, MINCED

ONE 12-OUNCE SIRLOIN OR NEW YORK STRIP STEAK

1 TABLESPOON FRESHLY GROUND BLACK PEPPER

1 ENGLISH CUCUMBER, CUT IN HALF LENGTHWISE AND THINLY SLICED

1 SMALL ONION, SLICED INTO RINGS

2 TOMATOES, SEEDED AND QUARTERED, OR ½ CUP CHERRY TOMATOES, HALVED

2 CUPS SEEDLESS GRAPES, HALVED

3 SCALLIONS, BOTH WHITE AND GREEN PARTS, CHOPPED

1 CUP FRESH CILANTRO LEAVES

1 CUP FRESH MINT LEAVES

1½ TABLESPOONS RICE POWDER (SEE COOK'S TIP)

1 TEASPOON HOT RED PEPPER FLAKES

1. To prepare the dressing, whisk together the lime juice, fish sauce, palm sugar syrup, and chiles in a bowl. Set aside.

2. Preheat the broiler. Coat the steak on both sides with the black pepper and put the steak in a baking pan. Broil the steak for about 3 minutes on each side for medium-rare. Remove from the oven and allow the meat to rest for 1 minute before slicing the steak very thinly across the grain. Place the sliced steak in a bowl and pour in half of the dressing.

3. In a salad bowl, combine the cucumber, onion, tomatoes, grapes, scallions, cilantro, mint, rice powder, and red pepper flakes. Add the remaining dressing and toss well.

4. To serve, arrange the beef on plates and top with the salad in the center. Drizzle with any remaining dressing from the salad bowl. Serve immediately.

Cook's Tip Rice powder adds an amazing crunchy texture to salads and is made by toasting uncooked jasmine rice and then grinding it. Put ¼ cup uncooked jasmine rice in a skillet over medium heat. Use a wooden spoon to stir the rice and cook until it appears golden brown, about 15 minutes. Transfer to a plate to cool. Grind the rice until the grains turn almost to powder using a mortar with a pestle or in a coffee or spice grinder. The results should resemble coarse cornmeal. The powder will keep for 1 month in an airtight glass jar.

Green Apple and Mango Salad

The mango, one of the most celebrated of tropical fruits, utters "forever summer" in my mind. For me, no other fruit is as magnificent as the mango. My memories of playing hide-and-seek with my cousins under our tree and eating the fruit between play are heavenly. In Malaysian Indian culture, the mango tree is a symbol of love and life; people believe that mango trees grow new leaves each time a son is born, so to announce a new birth, doorways are often decorated with mango leaves. Unripe mango is used in salads to complement a fried or grilled dish, particularly fish. In this salad the tartness of the green mango and apple is balanced by a touch of sugar. The pickled garlic, which you can find in jars at any Southeast Asian supermarket, adds a sweet crunch. SERVES 4

4 FRESH RED BIRD'S-EYE CHILES OR 2 SERRANO CHILES, FINELY CHOPPED

3 HEADS PICKLED GARLIC, CHOPPED

5 TABLESPOONS FRESH LIME JUICE

2 TEASPOONS FISH SAUCE

3 TEASPOONS PALM SUGAR SYRUP (PAGE 27) OR BROWN SUGAR

½ TEASPOON SALT

1 SMALL GREEN (UNRIPE) MANGO, PEELED AND SHREDDED

1 GREEN APPLE, PEELED, CORED, AND THINLY SLICED

3 SMALL SHALLOTS, FINELY SLICED

¼ CUP FRESH MINT LEAVES, FINELY CHOPPED

2 HARD-BOILED LARGE EGGS, PEELED AND SLICED

1 TABLESPOON GARLIC OIL (PAGE 31; OPTIONAL)

1. To prepare the dressing, combine the chiles, pickled garlic, lime juice, fish sauce, palm sugar syrup, and salt in a bowl. Mix well and set aside.

2. To prepare the salad, combine the mango, apple, shallots, and mint leaves in a bowl. Pour in the dressing and toss.

3. Arrange the salad on a serving platter and top with the sliced eggs. Drizzle with garlic oil if desired. Serve immediately.

Balinese Tuna Salad This recipe shows off the beauty of spice paste—it creates a lovely golden crust on the outside while enhancing the delicate taste of tuna. Every household in Bali has its own way of preparing this recipe; this is my version. Serve alone or accompanied by Tomato Sambal (page 202) and Cardamom Butter Rice with Sultanas (page 181) for a complete meal.

SERVES 4

FOUR 5-OUNCE AHI OR YELLOWFIN TUNA STEAKS, EACH ABOUT 1 INCH THICK

¼ CUP SEAFOOD SPICE PASTE (PAGE 62)

¼ CUP VEGETABLE OIL

2 TABLESPOONS FRESH LIME JUICE

2½ TEASPOONS SUGAR

½ TEASPOON SALT, OR TO TASTE

8 ROMAINE LETTUCE LEAVES, SHREDDED

1. Put the tuna steaks on a plate and coat evenly on both sides with the seafood spice paste.

2. Heat the oil in a small skillet over medium heat. Add the tuna to the pan and cook for 30 seconds on each side. The tuna should be cooked to medium. Remove and set aside.

3. Combine the lime juice, sugar, and salt in a medium bowl and whisk until the sugar is dissolved. Add the lettuce and toss well to coat.

4. To serve, arrange the lettuce on a serving plate. Slice the tuna into ½-inch-thick slices and arrange on top of the salad. Serve immediately.

Green Papaya Salad When I take my students on a culinary tour to a Southeast Asian market, the produce aisle is a popular stop. I am often asked how best to select a green papaya—an unripe papaya, oblong in shape. The fruit should be very firm to the touch. Green papaya is normally shredded and seasoned with lime juice, fish sauce, and palm sugar. Yard-long beans are pencil-thin legumes that resemble green beans except they are about 16 inches in length. They are light green in color, sweet, and more tender than green beans. Rich in vitamin A, they can be found year-round at most Asian markets and some supermarkets in the specialty produce section. They are tasty when eaten raw, blanched, or stir-fried.

Traditionally in Thailand, cooks use a wooden mortar to pound green papaya with dried shrimp, long beans, and tomatoes. I forgo the bruising in this salad to maintain its lovely crisp texture. This salad is best eaten cold, so you may make the dressing first and refrigerate it until ready to compose the salad. SERVES 4

3 TABLESPOONS FRESH LIME JUICE

3 TABLESPOONS FISH SAUCE

2½ TABLESPOONS PALM SUGAR SYRUP (PAGE 27) OR BROWN SUGAR

1 SMALL GREEN (UNRIPE) PAPAYA

5 GARLIC CLOVES

2 TO 3 SERRANO CHILES, TO TASTE, SLICED

1 TO 2 TABLESPOONS DRIED SHRIMP (OPTIONAL)

3 OUNCES YARD-LONG BEANS, CUT INTO ½-INCH LENGTHS

6 OUNCES CHERRY TOMATOES, HALVED

10 GREEN CABBAGE LEAVES, TORN INTO 2-INCH PIECES

5 TABLESPOONS UNSALTED ROASTED PEANUTS, CRUSHED

1. To prepare the dressing, combine the lime juice, fish sauce, and palm sugar syrup in a bowl. Cover and refrigerate for at least 15 minutes, or until ready to serve the salad.

2. Peel the papaya and cut it in half. Scoop the white seeds out with a spoon and discard. Shred the papaya with a grater. Grate only the green fruit, stopping when you come close to the inner white layer. Set aside.

3. Combine the garlic, chiles, and dried shrimp if you are using it in a mortar and mash with a pestle. Alternatively, you can use a food processor. Transfer to a medium bowl and add the papaya along with the long beans and tomatoes. Pour in the dressing and toss well.

4. To serve, place the salad on a serving plate and arrange the cabbage on the side. Garnish with peanuts. To eat, each person may use the cabbage to scoop up the papaya salad.

Spicy Seafood Salad

Spicy Seafood Salad This is a delicate and light-tasting dish, as the shrimp and squid are blanched to retain much of their fresh taste and texture. Fish sauce, fresh lime juice, palm sugar, and chiles are transformed into a classic sauce and combined with the seafood and aromatic herbs. You can prepare this dish with nearly any kind of seafood and serve with Perfect Jasmine Rice (page 176) on the side. Look for pickled garlic in jars at Southeast Asian markets. SERVES 4

¼ CUP FISH SAUCE

¼ CUP PLUS 1 TABLESPOON FRESH LIME JUICE

2½ TABLESPOONS PALM SUGAR SYRUP (PAGE 27) OR BROWN SUGAR

2 FRESH GREEN BIRD'S-EYE CHILES OR 1 SERRANO CHILE, CHOPPED

12 OUNCES MEDIUM SHRIMP, PEELED AND DEVEINED

12 OUNCES SQUID RINGS

1 SMALL WHITE ONION, THINLY SLICED

½ CUP FRESH MINT LEAVES

4 FRESH KAFFIR LIME LEAVES, STEMMED AND FINELY SLICED

2 HEADS PICKLED GARLIC, CHOPPED

1. To prepare the dressing, combine the fish sauce, lime juice, palm sugar syrup, and chiles in a small bowl and mix well. Set aside.

2. Bring a large saucepan or pot of water to a boil. Add the shrimp and boil for 2 minutes, or until pinkish orange. Remove the shrimp with a slotted spoon and set aside. Bring the water back to a boil. Add the squid and boil for 1 minute. Remove with a slotted spoon.

3. While the seafood is still warm, toss with the onion, mint, lime leaves, pickled garlic, and dressing in a medium serving bowl. Serve warm or at room temperature.

Apple and Radish Raita Raita is a raw vegetable or fruit salad that floats in a light creamy yogurt sauce. In this dish the combination of green apple and red radish provides crispness and a sweet and tart taste, while the cucumber offers a refreshing counterpoint to the lightly spiced yogurt. What's more, the burst of green and red makes a beautiful contrast. This salad is simple to prepare and should be served cold. MAKES ABOUT 4 CUPS

2 CUPS NONFAT YOGURT

1 GREEN APPLE, PEELED, CORED, AND DICED

1 CUP DICED RADISH

1 SMALL CUCUMBER, PEELED AND CHOPPED

1 TEASPOON CUMIN SEEDS

1 TEASPOON FENNEL SEEDS

1 TEASPOON SALT, OR TO TASTE

¼ TEASPOON FRESHLY GROUND BLACK PEPPER

½ CUP FRESH CILANTRO LEAVES, CHOPPED

1. Whisk the yogurt in a medium bowl until smooth. Add the apple, radish, and cucumber and mix well.

2. Toast the cumin and fennel in a small skillet over medium-low heat for 1 to 2 minutes, until aromatic and the cumin seeds have turned dark brown. Immediately remove the spices from the pan and pound them to a powder using a mortar and pestle. Alternatively, grind them in a coffee or spice grinder.

3. Add the spices, salt, and pepper to the yogurt mixture and stir to combine. Add the chopped cilantro. Cover and chill for at least 45 minutes or up to 1 hour before serving.

Pineapple, Jicama, and Green Mango with Tamarind Sauce

This salad is known as *rojak* and is my favorite snack whenever I am hungry. It is often sold from roadside stands. The rojak vendor combines sliced mango, pineapple, papaya, and a variety of other tropical fruits in season and tosses the ingredients in a tamarind and palm sugar sauce with crushed peanuts. A bamboo skewer is then used in place of a fork to eat this salad. Rojak is a great summertime salad, or it can be a healthy choice for dessert.

SERVES 4

½ CUP TAMARIND LIQUID (PAGE 35)

¼ TEASPOON SALT

¼ CUP PALM SUGAR SYRUP (PAGE 27) OR BROWN SUGAR

1 TEASPOON SHRIMP PASTE, TOASTED (PAGE 34)

3 TO 5 FRESH RED OR GREEN BIRD'S-EYE CHILES, TO TASTE, CHOPPED

1 SMALL FRESH PINEAPPLE, PEELED, CORED, AND CUT INTO 1-INCH PIECES

1 SMALL CUCUMBER, CHOPPED

½ SMALL JÍCAMA, PEELED AND CUT INTO 1-INCH PIECES

1 GREEN (UNRIPE) MANGO, PEELED AND SLICED

½ CUP CRUSHED UNSALTED ROASTED PEANUTS

1. To make the dressing, combine the tamarind liquid, salt, palm sugar syrup, shrimp paste, and chiles in a small saucepan over medium heat. Bring just to a boil. Immediately remove from the heat and set aside to cool.

2. Combine the pineapple, cucumber, jícama, and mango in a serving bowl. Add the dressing and peanuts and toss to coat. Serve immediately.

Fragrant Coconut Milk and Seafood
Soup

Somewhat mild and sweet, coconut milk soup tops my list of favorite Thai dishes. What makes it so heavenly is the bouquet of fresh aromatics such as lemongrass, galangal, and lime leaves, which infuse the coconut milk. Each spoonful is silky smooth and rich in flavor, aptly complementing the seafood. Most Southeast Asians enjoy this soup with a steaming bowl of rice. SERVES 4

TWO 14-OUNCE CANS COCONUT MILK (PAGE 26)

ONE 3-INCH PIECE FRESH GALANGAL, THINLY SLICED

8 FRESH KAFFIR LIME LEAVES, STEMMED AND THINLY SLICED

3 STALKS FRESH LEMONGRASS, BOTTOM PART ONLY, THINLY SLICED ON THE DIAGONAL

3 SHALLOTS, SLICED

3 TO 5 FRESH RED OR GREEN BIRD'S-EYE CHILES, TO TASTE, SLICED LENGTHWISE

12 MUSSELS, SCRUBBED AND DEBEARDED

8 OUNCES LARGE SHRIMP, PEELED AND DEVEINED

8 OUNCES SQUID RINGS

2 PLUM TOMATOES, CUT IN HALF AND SEEDED

2 TABLESPOONS FISH SAUCE, OR MORE TO TASTE

½ CUP FRESH CILANTRO LEAVES

2 SCALLIONS, BOTH WHITE AND GREEN PARTS, CHOPPED

3 TABLESPOONS FRESH LIME JUICE

1. Bring the coconut milk and ½ cup water just to a boil in a medium saucepan over medium heat. Add the galangal, lime leaves, lemongrass, shallots, and chiles, lower the heat, and cook for 20 minutes to release the aromatic oils, stirring occasionally.

2. Add the mussels, shrimp, squid, and tomatoes without stirring. Cover and cook for 1 minute.

3. Add the fish sauce, cilantro, and scallions and remove from the heat. Stir in the lime juice. Ladle into individual bowls and serve immediately.

Cook's Tip *You may strain the coconut milk to remove the aromatics before adding the seafood. However, when these ingredients are cut very thinly, I enjoy eating them as part of the soup.*

Split Yellow Lentil Soup

In the nineteenth century, Indian traders came to Malaya (now known as Malaysia after its independence from the British in 1957) in large numbers and brought with them their culinary staple: split lentils (toor dal). No Malaysian Indian meal is complete without dal. When I was a child, my mother would pour this smooth, slightly sweet, nutty-flavored lentil soup over hot rice and top it with a pat of butter, giving it a creamy taste. Now I do the same for my children. This dish is very versatile; eat it as a soup or enjoy it as part of a main meal. It is high in protein and fiber, cholesterol free, and easy to cook. I love to serve this with bread still warm from the oven or steamed Basmati Rice (page 177), with Green Apple and Nutmeg Chutney (page 196) on the side.

SERVES 4

1 CUP SPLIT YELLOW LENTILS (TOOR DAL)	¼ TEASPOON BLACK MUSTARD SEEDS
4 GARLIC CLOVES, MINCED	2 SPRIGS FRESH CURRY LEAVES
½ MEDIUM YELLOW ONION, MINCED	1 TEASPOON UNSALTED BUTTER (OPTIONAL)
¼ TEASPOON GROUND TURMERIC	
1½ TEASPOONS SALT, OR TO TASTE	2 TABLESPOONS CHOPPED FRESH CILANTRO LEAVES
1 TABLESPOON EXTRA VIRGIN OLIVE OIL	
¼ TEASPOON CUMIN SEEDS	

1. Wash the lentils by gently rubbing them with your fingers in a bowl under cold running until the water runs clear. Drain the lentils. Combine the lentils, garlic, onion, turmeric, and 5 cups water in a medium saucepan. Bring to a boil over medium heat, skimming off any foam that appears on the surface. Reduce the heat and simmer, stirring intermittently, until the lentils are soft and pureed, about 35 minutes. Season the lentils with salt.

2. Pour the olive oil into a small skillet over medium heat. When the oil is hot, add the cumin seeds, mustard seeds, and curry leaves. Immediately cover with a splatter screen to prevent the mustard seeds from popping out of the pan. After 30 seconds, the mustard seeds will start popping. When the mustard seeds stop popping, a few seconds more, turn off the heat and pour the oil and spices into the soup.

3. Cook the soup, stirring, for 3 minutes. Add the butter if you are using it and the cilantro and mix well. Remove from the heat and serve.

Hot and Sour Prawn Soup

Known as *tom yum kung*, this fragrant soup is distinctively Thai and is offered in every restaurant throughout Bangkok. The soup is characterized by its hotness from chiles, sourness from lime juice, saltiness from fish sauce, and sweetness from fresh aromatics like galangal and lemongrass. I always encourage my students to smell their hands moistened with essential oil after cutting the aromatics. The aromatics are elements that bring life to this soup. Roasted Chile Paste is added toward the end to give heat and bring together all the other flavors. Serve with Perfect Jasmine Rice (page 176) and Green Papaya Salad (page 94) for a classic Thai meal. SERVES 4

1 QUART CHICKEN BROTH

ONE 3-INCH PIECE FRESH GALANGAL, THINLY SLICED

8 FRESH KAFFIR LIME LEAVES, STEMMED AND TORN

4 STALKS FRESH LEMONGRASS, BOTTOM PART ONLY, THINLY SLICED ON THE DIAGONAL

5 TO 6 FRESH GREEN OR RED BIRD'S-EYE CHILES, TO TASTE, LIGHTLY CRUSHED

12 OUNCES MEDIUM PRAWNS OR JUMBO SHRIMP, PEELED AND DEVEINED

12 FRESH SHIITAKE MUSHROOMS, CAPS SLICED

1 TABLESPOON ROASTED CHILE PASTE (PAGE 61)

¼ CUP PLUS 2 TABLESPOONS FISH SAUCE, OR TO TASTE

¼ CUP FRESH LIME JUICE

½ CUP FRESH CILANTRO LEAVES

1. Bring the chicken broth just to a boil in a medium saucepan over medium heat. Add the galangal, lime leaves, lemongrass, and chiles. Cover and simmer over low heat for 15 minutes, stirring occasionally.

2. Add the prawns and mushrooms and cook for 1 minute. Stir in the chile paste and fish sauce. Taste, and if the soup is not salty enough, add more fish sauce. Remove from the heat and add the lime juice and cilantro. Serve immediately.

Vegetable Dishes

Green Beans and Carrots with Cumin Seeds

✦

Eggplant and Paneer in Spiced Tomato Sauce

✦

Stir-Fried Vegetables Thai Style

✦

Green Beans with Roasted Chile Paste

✦

Tofu in Sweet-Sour Sauce

✦

Red Curry with Bamboo Shoots, Tofu, and Zucchini

✦

Stir-Fried Bean Sprouts with White Pepper

✦

Chettinard Masala Potatoes

✦

Spiced Kabocha Squash

✦

Mild Coconut Curry with Tomatoes

✦

Stir-Fried Bok Choy and Shiitake Mushrooms
with Garlic

✦

Asparagus with Garlic and Rice Wine

Friday is vegetarian day in many Indian households, starting with early-morning prayers and myriad cleaning chores, followed by lunch with family or friends. At our home, when I was young, my mother's day would start with the first rays of light. Her faithful helper, the mango trader, would arrive on his bicycle, carting a bamboo basket full of freshly harvested vegetables and hand-picked mangoes. He literally had a little of everything from an entire garden: pumpkins, squash, green beans, carrots, bitter melon, tiny mushrooms, potatoes, and a mix of greens such as spinach and bok choy. It was my task to cut and clean these vegetables for our Friday catering to the customers at my mother's spice stall.

As she prepared the mashed pumpkin, tomatoes in coconut milk, and stir-fried vegetables, I was captivated by her deftness at pinching just the right amount of spices like cumin, anise, mustard seeds, or curry leaves to add to her dishes. Filling stainless-steel containers with vegetable dishes for the market, I would sneak a potato into my mouth and savor the warm curried flavors.

My mother's regular customers were Chettiars, or moneylenders, who through their many years of business dealings with her had become friends. The Chettiars came to Malaya as traders in whole spices. The local spice merchants combined the spices they bought from the Chettiars and resold them, often also taking out loans from the Chettiars to finance their ventures. At our spice stall, my mother would place several containers of her vegetable dishes in a basket and instruct me to bring them to the Chettiars' shops nearby. I was always greeted warmly by my mother's customers, who eagerly anticipated the vegetarian dishes she had cooked so lovingly.

The key to delicious vegetable dishes like those my mother prepared is the proper use of spices. In an Asian diet, rice is the base of all meals, but the principal focus is vegetables. Many are leafy greens that fill rows upon rows of shelves at most Asian grocery stores. Some fresh leafy greens may have a bland taste, but this is where herbs and spices play an important role. With the recipes in this chapter, you can take advantage of the endless selection of fresh leafy greens and other vegetables in season and expand your palate with healthy, delicious choices.

The following are spices that pair well with a variety of vegetables. As you cook with them, you will come to appreciate their unique flavors and become creative in using them. Most Southeast Asians do not measure spices; a pinch of this and a dash of that is the norm.

Mild Spices

✦ SWEET PAPRIKA—potatoes, squash, pumpkin, cauliflower, eggplant, sweet peppers

✦ CORIANDER—potatoes, pumpkin, eggplant, lentils

Hot Spices

✦ FRESH CHILES—carrots, green beans, spinach, bean sprouts, and just about all other vegetables

✦ BLACK AND WHITE PEPPER—all vegetables

✦ GINGER—potato, cauliflower, bamboo shoots, leafy greens, spinach, eggplant, tofu

✦ MUSTARD SEEDS—green beans, carrots, potato, squash, cauliflower, cucumber

Aromatic Dry Spices

✦ CUMIN—green beans, carrots, eggplant, potato, spinach, tomatoes, lentils, tofu

✦ ANISE SEEDS—potatoes, squash, eggplant, mushrooms

✦ FENNEL—potatoes, cauliflower, tofu

✦ FENUGREEK—lentils

✦ NUTMEG—potatoes, most summer and winter squash

✦ GROUND TURMERIC—potatoes, squash, tomatoes, cabbage

Aromatics

✦ GALANGAL—zucchini, bamboo shoots, tofu

✦ LEMONGRASS—zucchini, tomatoes, tofu, tempeh

✦ KAFFIR LIME LEAVES—tofu, eggplant, bamboo shoots

(continued)

✦ **CURRY LEAVES**—potatoes, tomatoes, cauliflower, turnips, green beans, carrots

✦ **SHALLOTS**—broccoli, green beans, carrots, eggplant, bean sprouts, potatoes, leafy greens

✦ **ONION**—all vegetables

✦ **GARLIC**—all vegetables

✦ **TURMERIC ROOT**—eggplant, turnips, okra, long beans, carrots, squash, bitter melon, tofu

Green Beans and Carrots with Cumin Seeds

This simple yet delectable vegetable dish is commonly served in Malaysian homes for lunch or dinner because it is a healthy addition to any meal. The mustard seeds and cumin release a warm, nutty flavor when added to hot oil, bringing out the very best in the vegetables. The natural sweetness of this dish beautifully complements Cardamom Butter Rice with Sultanas (page 181), served with salmon or any curry dish. SERVES 4

2 TABLESPOONS EXTRA VIRGIN OLIVE OIL

1 TEASPOON BLACK MUSTARD SEEDS

1 TEASPOON CUMIN SEEDS

2 GARLIC CLOVES, MINCED

2 LARGE SHALLOTS, FINELY CHOPPED

2 MEDIUM CARROTS, CUT INTO MATCHSTICKS

8 OUNCES GREEN BEANS, TRIMMED AND SLICED ON THE DIAGONAL

1 ½ TEASPOONS SALT, OR TO TASTE

1. Heat the olive oil in a large skillet over medium heat. Add the mustard and cumin seeds. Immediately cover with a splatter screen to prevent the mustard seeds from popping out of the pan. After 30 seconds, or when the mustard seeds just begin to pop, add the garlic and shallots. Cook, stirring occasionally, for 5 to 7 minutes, or until the shallots turn brown.

2. Add the carrots and green beans and cook until the vegetables are crisp-tender, 5 to 7 minutes. Season with salt and cook, stirring, for 1 minute. Remove from the heat and serve immediately.

Eggplant and Paneer in Spiced Tomato Sauce

I prepare this when I am seeking a hearty vegetarian dish. *Paneer* means "curd cheese," made by adding a curdling agent like lemon or vinegar to hot milk. The paneer used in this dish is a creamy cheese with a texture similar to that of fresh mozzarella. Paneer, which blends well with most ingredients, is sold at Indian grocery shops and many health food stores, but you can also use firm tofu. SERVES 4

½ CUP PLUS 2 TABLESPOONS EXTRA VIRGIN OLIVE OIL

1 FRESH GREEN CHILE, FINELY CHOPPED

ONE 1½-INCH PIECE FRESH GINGER, PEELED AND FINELY SLICED

3 GARLIC CLOVES, FINELY CHOPPED

1 TEASPOON GROUND CORIANDER

½ TEASPOON GROUND TURMERIC

2½ CUPS TOMATO SAUCE

5 TEASPOONS PALM SUGAR SYRUP (PAGE 27) OR BROWN SUGAR

1 TEASPOON SALT

1 SMALL EGGPLANT (10 TO 12 OUNCES), CUBED

12 OUNCES PANEER, CUBED

1. Heat 2 tablespoons of the olive oil in a medium saucepan over low heat. When the oil is hot, add the chile, ginger, and garlic and fry until the ginger is light brown and fragrant, about 2 minutes. Add the coriander and turmeric and sauté for a few seconds, stirring constantly.

2. Add the tomato sauce and season with the palm sugar syrup and salt. Cover and cook the sauce over low heat for 15 minutes, stirring occasionally.

3. While the sauce is cooking, heat ¼ cup of the remaining olive oil in a deep skillet over medium heat. Add the eggplant cubes without overcrowding the skillet and fry them until golden brown, turning once to cook the other side, about 4 minutes. Do not continuously stir the eggplant during this browning stage, or it will release too much moisture. Transfer the eggplant to paper towels to absorb any excess oil. Repeat the process until you have used all the eggplant.

4. In the same skillet, heat the remaining ¼ cup olive oil over medium-high heat. Add the paneer and cook until golden on all sides, turning occasionally, about 5 minutes.

5. Fold the cubes of paneer and the eggplant into the tomato sauce until they are entirely coated. Bring just to a boil. Remove from the heat and serve immediately.

Stir-Fried Vegetables Thai Style

Simple and quick to prepare, this dish is ideal for busy days. I love that the vegetables retain all their crunchiness and natural sweetness when tossed in a hot wok or large sauté pan. Feel free to add any vegetables of your choice to get as much variety out of this dish as possible. SERVES 4

¼ CUP CANOLA OR PEANUT OIL

3 GARLIC CLOVES, MINCED

2 CUPS BROCCOLI FLORETS

½ SMALL HEAD NAPA CABBAGE, COARSELY CHOPPED (ABOUT 1 ½ CUPS)

1 POUND SNOW PEAS, STEMMED

¼ CUP VEGETABLE BROTH

¼ CUP OYSTER SAUCE

1 TEASPOON ROASTED CHILE PASTE (PAGE 61)

½ TEASPOON SUGAR

Heat a wok or large nonstick sauté pan over medium heat for 40 seconds and then add the oil around the perimeter of the wok so that it coats the sides and bottom. When the surface shimmers slightly, after about 30 seconds, add the garlic and fry until golden, stirring constantly. Add the broccoli, cabbage, and snow peas and stir-fry for 2 minutes. Add the vegetable broth, oyster sauce, chile paste, and sugar and cook, stirring, until the snow peas are tender, about 2 minutes. Remove from the heat, transfer to a platter, and serve immediately.

Green Beans with Roasted Chile Paste

I distinctly remember how our neighbor would stroll into our home for a quick chat, help herself to some tea, and start to prepare beans, shallots, and chile paste for cooking. The time she saved us was truly invaluable. In my Seattle kitchen, to speed up my preparation, I always keep a bottle of roasted chile paste beside my stove. The wonder of this paste is that one teaspoon is all you need to transform green beans into a crunchy, exotic treat. SERVES 4

2 TABLESPOONS CANOLA OR PEANUT OIL	1 TABLESPOON SWEET SOY SAUCE
2 SHALLOTS, SLICED	1 TEASPOON ROASTED CHILE PASTE (PAGE 61)
1 POUND GREEN BEANS, TRIMMED AND SLICED ON THE DIAGONAL	SALT
1 TEASPOON SOY SAUCE	

Heat a wok or large nonstick sauté pan over medium heat for 40 seconds and then add the oil around the perimeter of the wok so that it coats the sides and bottom. When the surface shimmers slightly, after about 30 seconds, add the shallots and fry, stirring constantly, until golden brown, 2 to 3 minutes. Add the green beans and cook, stirring, for 2 minutes. Add the soy sauce, sweet soy sauce, and chile paste and cook, stirring, for 2 minutes. Add salt to taste and mix well. Remove from the heat, transfer to a platter, and serve immediately.

Cook's Tip This dish also tastes fabulous with zucchini and okra. When choosing okra, always look for pods that are young and crisp and be careful not to bruise or break them while washing.

Tofu in Sweet-Sour Sauce

Different from Chinese sweet and sour dishes in color and flavor, this recipe is distinctly Southeast Asian. The sweet and sour taste from the pineapple, the spiciness from onions and chiles, and the saltiness from fish sauce add layers of flavor during cooking. Serve this with a bowl of rice when you want a quick, light, healthy lunch. SERVES 4

¼ CUP CANOLA OR PEANUT OIL

ONE 14-OUNCE PACKAGE FIRM TOFU, DRAINED, PATTED DRY, AND CUBED

6 GARLIC CLOVES, MINCED

ONE 2-INCH PIECE FRESH GINGER, PEELED AND CUT INTO MATCHSTICKS

½ SMALL FRESH PINEAPPLE, PEELED, CORED, AND CUBED

1 RED BELL PEPPER, DICED

1 ½ CUPS SWEET-SOUR SAUCE (PAGE 65)

1 TABLESPOON TAPIOCA STARCH OR CORNSTARCH MIXED WITH 1 TABLESPOON WATER

1. Heat a wok or large nonstick sauté pan over low heat for 40 seconds and then add the oil around the perimeter of the wok so that it coats the sides and bottom. When the surface shimmers slightly, after about 40 seconds, add the tofu. Raise the heat to medium-high and fry until golden, turning once to cook the other side, about 12 minutes. If the tofu sticks to the pan, allow it to cook a little longer before stirring; it should come free once it browns. Transfer the tofu to paper towels to absorb any excess oil. Set the tofu aside. Save 1 tablespoon of the oil in the wok and discard the rest.

2. Heat the wok over medium-high heat. When the surface shimmers slightly, after about 30 seconds, add the garlic and ginger, and cook, stirring constantly, for about 2 minutes, or until golden brown. Raise the heat to high and add the fried tofu, pineapple, and bell pepper. Stir-fry for 5 minutes, searing the pineapple against the side of the hot wok to caramelize it.

3. Reduce the heat to medium, add the sweet-sour sauce, and cook, stirring, for 2 minutes. Add the tapioca starch mixture and continue to cook until the sauce thickens, about 1 minute. Remove from the heat and serve immediately.

Cook's Tip *Tapioca starch is made from the tubers of the cassava (yuca) plant. It is preferred as a sauce thickener in Asian cooking for its smooth mouthfeel and the fact that it thickens at a lower temperature than cornstarch.*

Red Curry with Bamboo Shoots, Tofu, and Zucchini

Young bamboo shoots, little known in Western cooking, are quite popular in dishes of Southeast Asian origin. In Malaysia, where this tropical plant grows in abundance, these shoots are harvested fresh at two weeks old, at about 1 foot in length, to be sold at markets. When cooked, fresh bamboo shoots taste like asparagus—sweet, crisp, and tender. However, for convenience, I have chosen to use canned bamboo shoots in this recipe. This recipe also uses store-bought fried tofu squares that come in a 12-ounce package, sold in the refrigerated section at all Asian supermarkets. The tofu is golden in color and has a meaty texture that complements the tender bamboo shoots and zucchini. If you can't find this tofu, use firm tofu instead. This is an exotic recipe, often called "the jungle prince." Serve with Perfect Jasmine Rice (page 176) and Tomato Sambal (page 202). SERVES 6

ONE 14-OUNCE CAN COCONUT MILK (PAGE 26)

1 TABLESPOON CILANTRO-GARLIC PASTE (PAGE 60)

¼ CUP THAI RED CURRY PASTE (PAGE 56 OR STORE-BOUGHT)

ONE 12-OUNCE PACKAGE FRIED TOFU, SLICED, OR ONE 16-OUNCE PACKAGE FIRM TOFU, DRAINED AND CUBED

2 SMALL ZUCCHINI, CHOPPED

TWO 8-OUNCE CANS SLICED BAMBOO SHOOTS, DRAINED AND RINSED

2 TABLESPOONS PALM SUGAR SYRUP (PAGE 27) OR BROWN SUGAR

2 FRESH RED CHILES, SEEDED AND THINLY SLICED

½ TEASPOON SALT, OR TO TASTE

⅓ CUP FRESH ASIAN SWEET BASIL LEAVES

---

1. Heat 1 cup of the coconut milk in a medium saucepan over medium heat. Bring just to a boil, then reduce the heat to medium-low and simmer, stirring frequently, until the oils from the coconut appear on the surface, about 7 minutes. Add the cilantro-garlic paste and red curry paste and mix well. Cook, stirring frequently, for about 7 minutes, until aromatic and the oils appear on the surface.

2. Add the remaining coconut milk, 1½ cups water, the tofu, zucchini, bamboo shoots, and palm sugar syrup. Cover and cook for 10 minutes. Add the chiles and salt and simmer for 10 minutes.

3. Rub the basil leaves between your hands to release the flavors and add to the pan. Stir once and remove from the heat. Serve immediately.

Stir-Fried Bean Sprouts with White Pepper

This dish, usually cooked with salted fish, is served at many restaurants in Malaysia for its simplicity and flavor. In this recipe, I have omitted the fish for the benefit of vegetarians. Simple and easy to prepare, the bean sprouts absorb all the delicate flavors from within the wok. SERVES 4

2 TABLESPOONS CANOLA OR PEANUT OIL

2 LARGE SHALLOTS, SLICED

1 POUND BEAN SPROUTS

2 FRESH RED CHILES, SEEDED AND CHOPPED

2 SCALLIONS, BOTH WHITE AND GREEN PARTS, CHOPPED

¼ TEASPOON FRESHLY GROUND WHITE PEPPER

1 TEASPOON SALT

¼ CUP FRESH CILANTRO LEAVES, ROUGHLY CHOPPED

Heat a wok or large nonstick sauté pan over medium heat for 40 seconds and then add the oil around the perimeter of the wok so that it coats the sides and bottom. When the surface shimmers slightly, after about 30 seconds, add the shallots and cook, stirring constantly, until golden brown, 3 to 4 minutes. Raise the heat to high and add the bean sprouts. Cook, stirring, for 30 seconds. Add the chiles, scallions, pepper, and salt and cook for 1 minute. Reduce the heat to medium, toss in the cilantro, and stir-fry for 30 seconds. Remove from the heat and serve immediately.

Chettinard Masala Potatoes

Cooked with curry leaves, turmeric, cumin, and mustard seeds until they take on a golden yellow color, these potatoes make a hearty and filling dish commonly served at vegetarian restaurants in Malaysia. This dish is not overpoweringly spicy, and therefore it can be consumed as an accompaniment to other curried, fried, or steamed dishes. This dish is lovely accompanied by Split Yellow Lentil Soup (page 100) and Green Beans and Carrots with Cumin Seeds (page 107). SERVES 4

1½ POUNDS MEDIUM RED POTATOES

3 TABLESPOONS EXTRA VIRGIN OLIVE OIL

½ TEASPOON MUSTARD SEEDS

½ TEASPOON ANISE SEEDS

3 SPRIGS FRESH CURRY LEAVES, STEMMED AND FINELY CHOPPED

1 FRESH GREEN CHILE, SEEDED AND FINELY SLICED

1 MEDIUM ONION, CHOPPED

1½ TABLESPOONS CURRY POWDER (PAGE 44 OR 45 OR STORE-BOUGHT)

½ TEASPOON GROUND TURMERIC

1 TEASPOON PURE CHILE POWDER (PAGE 17) OR CAYENNE

1½ TEASPOONS SALT, OR TO TASTE

1. Put the potatoes in a large pot of cold water over medium heat. Bring to a simmer and cook until the potatoes are tender, about 30 minutes. Drain the potatoes and allow them to cool slightly. Peel and cut into 1-inch cubes.

2. Heat the oil in a medium skillet over medium heat. When the oil is hot, add the mustard seeds and immediately cover with a splatter screen to prevent the mustard seeds from popping out of the pan. When the mustard seeds just begin to pop, after about 30 seconds, add the anise seeds, curry leaves, chile, and onion. Sauté until the onion becomes translucent and light brown, about 3 minutes.

3. Add the curry powder, turmeric, and chile powder and mix well. Add the potatoes and cook, mixing gently every few minutes, until golden brown, about 10 minutes. Stir in the salt and mix well. Serve immediately.

Spiced Kabocha Squash

I might as well call this dish "Pumpkin Friday," because no Friday would have been complete when I was growing up unless the whole family had relished this sweet goodness. I use kabocha squash in this recipe as it is naturally sweeter than most squash and not stringy. It has a similar taste to that of the sweet potato and is available year-round. I am often asked to demonstrate the preparation of this dish at the farmers' market in the Seattle metro area. It's always a hit with the crowd. If you cannot find kabocha squash, use buttercup instead. This dish is lovely accompanied by Split Yellow Lentil Soup (page 100) and a plate of Basmati Rice (page 177).

SERVES 4

ONE 2-POUND KABOCHA SQUASH, QUARTERED AND SEEDED

3 TABLESPOONS EXTRA VIRGIN OLIVE OIL

½ TEASPOON MUSTARD SEEDS

½ TEASPOON CUMIN SEEDS

ONE 1-INCH PIECE FRESH GINGER, PEELED AND THINLY SLICED

1 MEDIUM ONION, CHOPPED

3 TO 5 DRIED RED CHILES, TO TASTE, BROKEN IN HALF

1½ TABLESPOONS CURRY POWDER (PAGE 44 OR 45 OR STORE-BOUGHT)

½ TEASPOON GROUND TURMERIC

1½ TEASPOONS SALT, OR TO TASTE

1. Bring water to a boil in the bottom of a steamer over medium heat. Put the squash in the steamer insert and place over the boiling water. Cover and cook the squash until tender and moist, about 10 minutes. Alternatively, you may steam the squash by placing it in a pan with ½ cup water. Cover with a tight-fitting lid and cook over medium heat for 10 minutes. Drain and set aside to cool. Peel and cut the flesh into 1-inch cubes.

2. Heat the oil in a large skillet over medium heat. Add the mustard seeds, cumin seeds, ginger, onion, and dried chiles and stir until the onion becomes translucent, 4 to 5 minutes. Add the curry powder and turmeric and cook for 2 minutes.

3. Add the squash and salt and stir gently. Cook for 2 minutes. Remove from the heat and serve immediately.

Mild Coconut Curry with Tomatoes

This is a curry my mother used to cook for my brother and me when we were children. I remember helping her squeeze fresh coconut milk for this dish, which we called *sothy*. We loved this curry and ate it several times a week, always with a different green vegetable or tofu. My children also love it, and I feel content every time I make this curry, which is filled with a rainbow of vitamins and mild flavors to stimulate their appetites, especially in the heat of the summer. Serve with steamed Basmati Rice (page 177) and Chettinard Masala Potatoes (page 114) and chutneys of your choice. SERVES 6

3 TABLESPOONS EXTRA VIRGIN OLIVE OIL

½ TEASPOON MUSTARD SEEDS

½ TEASPOON CUMIN SEEDS

2 SPRIGS FRESH CURRY LEAVES

2 GARLIC CLOVES, MINCED

2 LARGE SHALLOTS, MINCED

2 LARGE RIPE TOMATOES, QUARTERED

ONE 14-OUNCE CAN COCONUT MILK (PAGE 26)

½ TEASPOON GROUND TURMERIC

½ TEASPOON SALT, OR TO TASTE

1. Heat the oil in a medium saucepan over medium heat. Add the mustard seeds, cumin seeds, curry leaves, garlic, shallots, and tomatoes and stir until the mixture is aromatic and the tomatoes are soft, about 7 minutes.

2. Add the coconut milk, ½ cup water, the turmeric, and the salt and bring just to a boil. Remove from the heat and serve hot or warm.

Stir-Fried Bok Choy and Shiitake Mushrooms with Garlic

Bok choy, the Asian green, is loaded with vitamin C, beta-carotene, and fiber. I love this recipe because it's quick and preserves all the vegetable's nutrients, as well as its crunchiness and bright green color. SERVES 4

---

1 POUND BOK CHOY

3 TABLESPOONS CANOLA OR PEANUT OIL

4 GARLIC CLOVES, MINCED

8 MEDIUM SHIITAKE MUSHROOM CAPS, SLICED

2½ TABLESPOONS OYSTER SAUCE

¼ CUP CHICKEN BROTH

---

1. Separate the bok choy leaves from the stems and wash the leaves thoroughly under running water. Drain well and set aside.

2. Heat a wok or large nonstick sauté pan over medium heat for 40 seconds and then add the oil around the perimeter of the wok so that it coats the sides and bottom. When the surface shimmers slightly, after about 30 seconds, add the garlic. Cook, stirring constantly, until the garlic is golden, about 1 minute. Raise the heat to high and add the bok choy and shiitake mushrooms. Cook, stirring and placing the garlic on top of the vegetables to prevent it from burning, for 2 minutes. Add the oyster sauce and chicken broth and continue to cook for 1 minute. Remove from the heat and serve immediately.

Asparagus with Garlic and Rice Wine

I love the taste of asparagus when it's cooked lightly with garlic, chile, and rice wine. Asparagus reminds me of a particular vegetable called "Sabah veggie" from Lahad Datu, in the state of Sabah in East Malaysia. This easy recipe emphasizes the sweet taste of asparagus in less than 5 minutes, making it a perfect weeknight side dish. SERVES 4

3 TABLESPOONS CANOLA OR PEANUT OIL

1 POUND ASPARAGUS, TRIMMED AND CUT INTO 2-INCH LENGTHS

¼ TEASPOON SALT, OR TO TASTE

¼ TEASPOON FRESHLY GROUND WHITE PEPPER

4 GARLIC CLOVES, MINCED

1 FRESH RED OR GREEN CHILE, SEEDED AND MINCED

1 TABLESPOON RICE WINE

¼ CUP CHICKEN BROTH

1 TABLESPOON SOY SAUCE

1. Heat a wok or large nonstick sauté pan over medium heat for 40 seconds and then add the oil around the perimeter of the wok so that it coats the sides and bottom. When the surface shimmers slightly, after about 30 seconds, add the asparagus, salt and pepper. Cook, stirring, for 1 minute. Add the garlic and chile and cook, stirring, for 1 minute.

2. Add the rice wine, chicken broth, and soy sauce. Raise the heat to medium-high and continue to cook for 2 minutes, until the asparagus is crisp-tender. Remove from the heat and serve immediately.

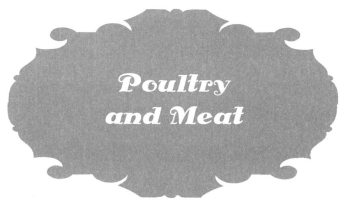

Poultry and Meat

Basil Chicken

✦

Whole Roasted Chicken in Tamarind Butter Sauce

✦

Stir-Fried Chicken with Cashews

✦

Merchant's Fried Chicken

✦

Chicken Curry

✦

Tender Beef Curry with Potatoes

✦

Spiced Rubbed Beef Short Ribs

✦

Marinated Sirloin with Black Pepper and Coriander

✦

Trader's Beef Massaman Curry

✦

Lamb Chops Parratal

✦

Lamb Korma

✦

Braised Pork in Caramelized Soy Sauce

✦

Thai Green Pork Curry

Sunday was always a special day for my family: this was the day that my father would show off his prowess in the kitchen. It would all start with a drive to Brickfields.

Brickfields, its name left behind by the colonials, was a spice merchants' enclave close to Bangsar, where we lived. A suburb overlooked in the country's tourist guidebook, Brickfields was where Naina Baba, the community butcher and a good friend of my father's, had his shop squeezed into a corner, sharing space with a store that sold trinkets from India. Hailing us with a warm "hello" from behind pieces of mutton hung on hooks, he would cut choice selections using a cleaver on a round upright tree stump. My father would always bring several bottles of my mother's mango chutney and lime pickles for him in exchange.

As we made our way back, my father would talk excitedly about how he planned to prepare the lamb and chicken that afternoon. When we arrived home, our arms full of groceries, we would quickly lay the produce on the table of our kitchen. Dad would roll up his sleeves and grind the chiles, ginger, and garlic for the lamb korma in our weathered stone mortar and marinate the chicken with ground chile, turmeric, and salt for merchant's fried chicken. The ripe tomatoes from our garden were washed and chopped, curry leaves plucked from our tree in the backyard, and a variety of spices were combined on a large plate to be added to various pots.

Around 2:00 P.M., a lavish spread would sit on our long dining table covered in voile cloth that had belonged to my grandmother: beef biryani, lamb korma, fried chicken, curried potatoes, mixed vegetables, lamb chops in lentil curry (*dalcha*), and more. My father's cooking and sharing of food with our extended family was nothing less than a labor of love.

Here in my Seattle kitchen, I continue to cook and share Sunday lunch on a smaller scale with my family and friends. The dishes in this chapter, such as Whole Roasted Chicken in Tamarind Butter Sauce, Basil Chicken, Thai Green Pork Curry, Tender Beef Curry with Potatoes, and Lamb Korma, make a perfect feast.

Basil Chicken

Basil, also known as *tulasi*, is often seen in home gardens of Indian families in Malaysia. It is regarded as one of the most sacred plants of Indian culture. In this dish, the basil releases bursts of sweet licorice-like flavor a few seconds after it is added to the wok. When making this dish, the key is to keep the chicken pieces small so the sauce penetrates the meat. SERVES 4

¼ CUP CANOLA OR PEANUT OIL

6 GARLIC CLOVES, MINCED

2 SMALL SHALLOTS, THINLY SLICED

4 FRESH GREEN OR RED BIRD'S-EYE CHILES OR 2 SERRANO CHILES, CHOPPED

1 ½ POUNDS BONELESS, SKINLESS CHICKEN BREAST, CUT INTO ¾-INCH PIECES

2 TABLESPOONS SWEET SOY SAUCE

3 TABLESPOONS FISH SAUCE

1 ½ CUPS FIRMLY PACKED FRESH ASIAN SWEET BASIL LEAVES, TORN INTO PIECES

¼ TEASPOON FRESHLY GROUND WHITE PEPPER

1. Heat a wok or large nonstick sauté pan over medium heat for 40 seconds and then add the oil around the perimeter of the wok so that it coats the sides and bottom. When the surface shimmers slightly, after about 30 seconds, add the garlic, shallots, and chiles and cook, stirring constantly, until light golden, 3 to 4 minutes. Add the chicken and cook until the chicken is almost no longer pink on the inside, about 10 minutes.

2. Raise the heat to medium-high and add the sweet soy sauce and fish sauce. Cook, stirring, until the chicken is completely cooked, about 3 minutes. Add the basil and pepper and cook for a few seconds. Remove from the heat and serve immediately.

Whole Roasted Chicken in Tamarind Butter

Sauce My mother was celebrated for her roasted chicken, which was tender and flavorful right to the bone. She first made this recipe for one of our regular customers at our spice stall and soon enough could hardly keep up with the orders. I enjoyed standing beside her as she made it, watching the palm sugar, butter, and tamarind as they caramelized. In this recipe, we never used the reserved juices from the pan as the tamarind sauce was so delicious on its own. However, you may serve the reserved sauce on the side if you wish. Just before serving, my mother would sprinkle in a handful of fried chiles for an extra kiss of flavor. SERVES 6

Chicken
2 TEASPOONS CORIANDER SEEDS

4 STAR ANISE

ONE 4-INCH CINNAMON STICK

2 GARLIC CLOVES, PEELED

⅓ CUP SOY SAUCE

ONE 4½- TO 5-POUND WHOLE CHICKEN

Sauce
1 TABLESPOON UNSALTED BUTTER

½ CUP PLUS 2 TABLESPOONS TAMARIND LIQUID (PAGE 35)

2 TABLESPOONS FISH SAUCE

¼ CUP SOY SAUCE

½ CUP PALM SUGAR SYRUP (PAGE 27) OR BROWN SUGAR

½ TEASPOON CAYENNE

1. To prepare the marinade, put the coriander, star anise, and cinnamon in a skillet over medium-low heat. Cook for 1 to 2 minutes, until fragrant and slightly darkened. Set aside to cool.

2. Put the toasted spices, garlic, and soy sauce in a food processor or mini-chopper. Blend until you have a smooth paste.

3. Put the chicken in a glass baking dish and pour the marinade over the chicken, rubbing inside and out with the spices. Cover and refrigerate for at least 6 hours, preferably overnight.

4. Preheat the oven to 375°F. Put the chicken on a rack, reserving the marinade, and then place the rack on top of a baking pan. Fill the pan with ½ inch of water.

Roast the chicken for 1 hour, basting the chicken with the reserved marinade every 20 minutes.

5. Roast for 30 minutes longer without basting, until the juices run clear when you prick the thigh with a fork. Remove the chicken from the oven and allow to rest for 10 minutes before carving.

6. While the chicken is resting, put a saucepan over medium heat. Add the butter, tamarind liquid, fish sauce, soy sauce, and ¼ cup water and bring to a boil. Add the palm sugar syrup and cayenne, stirring gently to dissolve the sugar. Bring to a boil and cook for 3 minutes, until the sauce is deep reddish brown in color and slightly thickened.

7. Carve the chicken, arrange the pieces on a platter, and pour the sauce over them.

Stir-Fried Chicken with Cashews Cashew nuts are

popular in Southeast Asian cooking, adding both taste and texture to many stir-fried dishes. It is believed that the cashew nut tree originated in southeastern Brazil and that seedlings reached India in the early sixteenth century. The Portuguese, themselves ardent adventurers plying the old trade routes, first brought cashew nut trees to Malaysia, planting them in the sandy east coast of the peninsula close to the Thai border. Today, due to their abundance, cashew nuts find their way into many dishes like this tasty cashew chicken cooked in roasted chile paste. SERVES 4

5 TABLESPOONS CANOLA OR PEANUT OIL

8 GARLIC CLOVES, MINCED

1 ½ POUNDS BONELESS, SKINLESS CHICKEN BREAST, CUT INTO ¾-INCH PIECES

⅓ CUP ROUGHLY BROKEN DRIED RED CHILES

¼ CUP OYSTER SAUCE

3 TABLESPOONS ROASTED CHILE PASTE (PAGE 61)

1 TABLESPOON FISH SAUCE, OR TO TASTE

1 CUP UNSALTED ROASTED CASHEWS

4 SCALLIONS, BOTH WHITE AND GREEN PARTS, CUT INTO 1-INCH PIECES

1. Heat a wok or large nonstick sauté pan over medium heat for 40 seconds and then add the oil around the perimeter of the wok so that it coats the sides and bottom. When the surface shimmers slightly, after about 30 seconds, add the garlic and cook, stirring constantly, until light golden, 2 minutes. Add the chicken and cook until no longer pink on the outside but not fully cooked, about 7 minutes. Move the chicken to one side of the wok and add the chiles to the center. Cook the chiles until darkened, 2 to 3 minutes.

2. Bring the chicken to the center of the wok and continue to cook until the chicken browns evenly, about 5 minutes. Add the oyster sauce, chile paste, fish sauce, and cashews and cook for 2 minutes.

3. Raise the heat to high, toss in the scallions, and cook for 30 seconds. Remove from the heat and serve immediately.

Merchant's Fried Chicken

Fried chicken is extremely popular in Southeast Asian marketplaces, where spice merchants try to outdo each other and convince customers that their chicken tastes the best. This recipe, passed down to me by my mother, uses a select mix of spices. Never oily, Merchant's Fried Chicken is crusty and crunchy on the outside, juicy and tender on the inside—a wholesome meal for hungry kids and adults. SERVES 4

ONE 4-POUND WHOLE CHICKEN, CUT INTO 12 PIECES (SEE COOK'S TIP)

1 TEASPOON PURE CHILE POWDER (PAGE 17) OR CAYENNE

1 TEASPOON GROUND TURMERIC

1 TEASPOON GROUND FENNEL

2 TEASPOONS SALT, OR TO TASTE

CANOLA OIL FOR FRYING

3 TABLESPOONS POTATO STARCH OR CORNSTARCH

1. Put the chicken pieces in a large bowl and sprinkle with the chile powder, turmeric, fennel, and salt. Rub the chicken thoroughly with the spices. Cover and refrigerate for at least 3 hours or overnight.

2. Heat 4 inches of oil in a large wok or nonstick sauté pan over medium-high heat. Meanwhile, sprinkle the potato starch over the chicken to coat the chicken well.

3. When the oil is hot (you may test the oil with a chopstick: if the oil bubbles around the stick, the oil is ready), add the chicken, a few pieces at a time, without overcrowding the wok. Cook for 12 to 15 minutes, until thoroughly cooked and golden brown. Drain on paper towels and repeat with the remaining chicken pieces, taking care to bring the oil back to the appropriate temperature before adding each batch. Serve hot.

Cook's Tip *The smaller you cut up the chicken, the better the spices can penetrate the meat, which will cook quickly and evenly. To get twelve pieces, separate the wings from the chicken, and then cut the breasts into two or three pieces each. Separate the drumsticks from the thighs and cut the thighs crosswise in half to make two pieces each.*

Chicken Curry

Chicken Curry The most wonderful thing about making this curry is the heavenly fragrance that drifts through the house when the spices are being cooked. This is my family's recipe, and it has been with us for a long time. We use our Fiery Curry Powder for Meat to provide the heat from dried chiles and to achieve an appealing red gravy. If you are making this curry for kids, go very light on the curry powder and up the amount of potatoes to three or four for a mild and creamy texture. I recommend opting for dark meat with the bone as it makes for a tastier gravy. At home, with the curry this good, we could care less about the meat—everyone's *really* after the gravy. SERVES 6

- -

2 POUNDS BONE-IN CHICKEN PIECES

¼ CUP PLUS 1 TABLESPOON EXTRA VIRGIN OLIVE OIL

2 SPRIGS FRESH CURRY LEAVES

TWO 3-INCH CINNAMON STICKS

1 STAR ANISE

¼ TEASPOON CLOVES

3 GREEN CARDAMOM PODS, CRUSHED

1 LARGE RED ONION, CHOPPED

2 TABLESPOONS GINGER-GARLIC PASTE (PAGE 59)

1 MEDIUM POTATO, PEELED AND QUARTERED

2 TOMATOES, QUARTERED

1 TEASPOON GROUND TURMERIC

½ TO 1 TABLESPOON CURRY POWDER (PAGE 44 OR 45 OR STORE-BOUGHT)

1 ½ TEASPOONS SALT, OR TO TASTE

⅓ CUP CANNED COCONUT MILK (PAGE 26)

- -

1. Cut the chicken thighs in half crosswise with a cleaver or, if using breasts, cut each one into 4 or 5 pieces. Set aside.

2. Heat the oil in a large pot over medium heat. When the oil is hot, add the curry leaves (make sure the curry leaves are dry or they will splatter the oil), cinnamon, star anise, cloves, and cardamom pods. Stir and cook until fragrant, about 2 minutes. Add the onion and cook until translucent and light brown, about 7 minutes. Add the ginger-garlic paste, stir, and cook for 1 minute.

3. Add the chicken, potato, tomatoes, turmeric, and curry powder and mix well. Cover, turn the heat to medium-low, and cook, stirring occasionally, for

35 minutes, until the potatoes and chicken pieces are tender. (If you prefer your curry to have a thick sauce, do not cover the pot.)

4. Add the salt and coconut milk, stirring to mix thoroughly. Cook for 10 minutes, or until a little oil appears on the surface. Remove from the heat and serve hot.

Cook's Tip *When making any curry, you may choose to make it "wet," with lots of gravy, or "dry," with a minimal amount of gravy. If you prefer lots of gravy, keep the pot covered while the curry simmers. If you desire thick gravy, leave the pot uncovered and allow the liquid in the curry to evaporate as the curry cooks.*

Tender Beef Curry with Potatoes
This is one of my favorite recipes for stewed meat curry. In Malaysia, my family would make this recipe with lamb on Sundays, but beef tastes just as good, cooked over low heat to tenderize it properly. When you make this curry, don't skip the curry leaves. During my cooking classes, I pass around a sprig of fresh curry leaves selected from my local Indian grocery shop. When my students rub the leaves between their fingers and the sensational oils are released, they realize the fragrance it brings to the curry. Cinnamon, star anise, cloves, onions, and tomatoes cooked with the beef make this a hearty dish. If you have any left over, the curry actually tastes better the next day. Enjoy this dish with Cardamom Butter Rice with Sultanas (page 181) and Green Mango Chutney (page 194) on the side.

SERVES 6

¼ CUP PLUS 2 TABLESPOONS CANOLA OIL

TWO 4-INCH CINNAMON STICKS

2 STAR ANISE

2 CLOVES

¼ CUP GINGER-GARLIC PASTE (PAGE 59)

½ CUP FRESH CURRY LEAVES

2 MEDIUM RED ONIONS, ROUGHLY CHOPPED

5 MEDIUM TOMATOES, CUT IN HALF

2 TEASPOONS GROUND TURMERIC

1½ TABLESPOONS GROUND CORIANDER

2 POUNDS BONELESS BEEF CHUCK, CUT INTO 1½-INCH CUBES

3 TO 4 MEDIUM RED POTATOES, PEELED AND QUARTERED

2 TO 3 TABLESPOONS CURRY POWDER (PAGE 44 OR 45 OR STORE-BOUGHT), TO TASTE

2 TEASPOONS PURE CHILE POWDER (PAGE 17) OR CAYENNE, OR TO TASTE

SALT

3 TABLESPOONS CHOPPED FRESH CILANTRO LEAVES

1. Heat the oil in a large heavy pot or Dutch oven over medium heat. Add the cinnamon, star anise, cloves, ginger-garlic paste, and curry leaves and cook until the spices are aromatic, about 1 minute. Add the onions and cook until soft and translucent, about 15 minutes.

2. Add the tomatoes, stir well to combine, and cook for 3 minutes, until the tomatoes begin to break down. Add the turmeric, coriander, beef, and 1 cup water. Stir and bring to a boil over medium heat. Reduce the heat to low and simmer, covered, stirring occasionally to prevent burning, for 1 hour, until the beef is tender.

3. Add the potatoes, curry powder, and chile and stir well. Cover and cook until the potatoes are tender, about 15 minutes. Season with salt to taste and stir well to combine.

4. Raise the heat to medium, uncover the pot, and bring to a boil without stirring until the oil separates and appears on the surface. Remove from the heat and garnish with cilantro. Serve hot.

Spiced Rubbed Beef Short Ribs

This dish takes only 10 minutes to cook but tastes like you've labored in the kitchen for hours. I use thin-cut beef short ribs, as they cook fast without getting tough. This cut is sold in all Asian supermarkets and many gourmet markets as "teriyaki cut beef short ribs." This dish reminds me of my summer days in Ala Moana Beach Park in Hawaii, where I would grill short ribs on the beach on my little hibachi. SERVES 6

2½ POUNDS THIN-CUT BEEF SHORT RIBS

2 TABLESPOONS GINGER-GARLIC PASTE
(PAGE 59)

2 TABLESPOONS STEAK AND CHOP RUB
(PAGE 52)

½ CUP WORCESTERSHIRE SAUCE

1 TEASPOON SUGAR

2 TABLESPOONS EXTRA VIRGIN OLIVE OIL

1. Put the short ribs in a large bowl. Add the ginger-garlic paste, steak and chop rub, Worcestershire sauce, and sugar and rub all over the meat until well coated. Cover and refrigerate for 3 hours before cooking.

2. When ready to cook, heat the oil in a large skillet over medium heat. When hot, add the beef short ribs in a single layer, as many as the pan will hold. Cook until browned, about 5 minutes on each side. Remove from the heat and transfer to a serving plate. Repeat with the remaining ribs. Serve immediately.

Marinated Sirloin with Black Pepper and Coriander

This is a superb dish if you want a meal in a jiffy. Sirloin is coated with black peppercorns, coriander, and sweet soy sauce and stir-fried with heady ginger and chiles to make this dish exotic, a blending of Indian and Chinese flavors. You may use flank steak in place of sirloin if you prefer. To ensure the cooking time is short, have all your ingredients ready and make sure your wok is hot before you start. SERVES 4

1 POUND BONELESS BEEF SIRLOIN, THINLY SLICED

¼ CUP SOY SAUCE

2 TABLESPOONS SWEET SOY SAUCE

2 TEASPOONS BLACK PEPPERCORNS, CRUSHED

1 TEASPOON CORIANDER SEEDS, CRUSHED

2 TABLESPOONS CORNSTARCH

3 TABLESPOONS CANOLA OR PEANUT OIL

1 SMALL WHITE ONION, HALVED AND THINLY SLICED

ONE 3-INCH PIECE FRESH GINGER, PEELED AND CUT INTO MATCHSTICKS

1 TO 2 FRESH GREEN OR RED CHILES, TO TASTE, THINLY SLICED

1 TEASPOON SALT, OR TO TASTE

3 SCALLIONS, BOTH WHITE AND GREEN PARTS, CHOPPED

1. Combine the meat, soy sauce, sweet soy sauce, peppercorns, coriander seeds, and cornstarch in a bowl. Mix well to combine the flavors. Set aside for 15 minutes to marinate.

2. Heat a wok or large nonstick sauté pan over medium heat for 40 seconds and then add the oil around the perimeter of the wok so that it coats the sides and bottom. When the surface shimmers slightly, after about 30 seconds, add the onion and ginger and cook, stirring, until the onion is translucent, about 5 minutes.

3. Raise the heat to high, add the meat, and cook, stirring and searing the meat against the side of the hot wok, about 12 minutes.

4. Toss in the chiles, salt, and scallions and cook for 1 minute. Remove from the heat and serve immediately.

Trader's Beef Massaman Curry

This is my version of the Massaman curry sold by Nasi Kandar restaurants in Penang, an island situated on the northwest coast of Peninsular Malaysia. These restaurants are extremely popular because they bring a unique combination of tastes: hot, spicy curries prepared from traditional Indian recipes, but with the favors tweaked for Thai taste buds. If you have any left over, this succulent beef curry will taste even better the next day. SERVES 6

3 TABLESPOONS EXTRA VIRGIN OLIVE OIL

3 SHALLOTS, QUARTERED

4 GREEN CARDAMOM PODS, CRUSHED

1 STAR ANISE

⅓ CUP THAI MASSAMAN CURRY PASTE (PAGE 58 OR STORE-BOUGHT)

3 POUNDS BONELESS BEEF CHUCK, SLICED 2 INCHES THICK ACROSS THE GRAIN

4 MEDIUM RED POTATOES, PEELED AND CUT IN HALF

1 CUP COCONUT MILK (PAGE 26)

¼ CUP PLUS 2 TABLESPOONS TAMARIND LIQUID (PAGE 35)

3 TABLESPOONS PALM SUGAR SYRUP (PAGE 27) OR BROWN SUGAR

2 TABLESPOONS FISH SAUCE, OR TO TASTE

10 TO 12 DRIED RED CHILES, TO TASTE

¼ CUP UNSALTED ROASTED PEANUTS

1. Heat the oil in a large heavy pot or Dutch oven over medium heat. Add the shallots, cardamom pods, star anise, and curry paste. Cook, stirring, until the shallots are soft and the paste is fragrant, about 5 minutes.

2. Raise the heat to medium-high and add the meat and potatoes. Mix for a minute, until the meat is coated with the spices. Add ½ cup water, cover, and simmer over medium heat for 10 minutes.

3. Stir in the coconut milk, tamarind liquid, palm sugar syrup, fish sauce, and chiles. Cover, reduce the heat to medium-low, and cook for 20 minutes.

4. Add the peanuts, uncover, and simmer until the meat is tender, about 30 minutes, stirring every so often. Remove from the heat. Serve hot.

Lamb Chops Parratal

Parratal is a dish similar to the one in India called *rogan josh*. The word *parratal* means "dry curry." This recipe, red from the ground dried chile, is probably the best loved of all curries among Indians in Malaysia. When I am in Malaysia visiting family, I make sure this is the first curry I savor when I arrive and the last before I leave. It goes very well with Basmati Rice (page 177) or Saffron Pilaf (page 180). SERVES 4

¼ CUP PLUS 2 TABLESPOONS CANOLA OR PEANUT OIL

TWO 2-INCH CINNAMON STICKS

5 GREEN CARDAMOM PODS, CRUSHED

1 STAR ANISE

4 CLOVES

2 SMALL RED ONIONS, ROUGHLY CHOPPED

1 FRESH GREEN CHILE, SEEDED AND SLICED LENGTHWISE

2 TABLESPOONS GINGER-GARLIC PASTE (PAGE 59)

2 SPRIGS FRESH CURRY LEAVES

3 MEDIUM TOMATOES, QUARTERED

2 POUNDS BONE-IN LAMB SHOULDER, CUT INTO 3-INCH PIECES

¼ TEASPOON GROUND TURMERIC

2 TABLESPOONS PURE CHILE POWDER (PAGE 17) OR CAYENNE

1 TEASPOON SALT, OR TO TASTE

¼ CUP YOGURT

1. Heat the oil in a large heavy pot or Dutch oven over medium heat. Add the cinnamon, cardamom pods, star anise, and cloves and cook until fragrant, about 1 minute. Add the onions, green chile, ginger-garlic paste, and curry leaves. Cook, stirring until the onions are soft, about 10 minutes.

2. Add the tomatoes, lamb, turmeric, and chile powder and give it a good stir. Cover and simmer over low heat, stirring occasionally, until the meat is tender, about 30 minutes.

3. Season with salt to taste. Add the yogurt and stir until well blended. Uncover and cook over medium heat for 15 minutes, until thick. Remove from the heat and serve hot.

Lamb Korma This dish has *celebration* written all over it. When I was a child, no birthday, Christmas, New Year, or even Sunday was complete without korma, a thick, mild, creamy curry that gets its flavor and texture from ground cashew nuts. Korma is bound to please everyone, adults and children alike. You can vary this recipe with chicken, lamb, or vegetables—the choice is entirely yours. This dish is grand served with Saffron Pilaf (page 180). SERVES 4

¼ CUP PLUS 2 TABLESPOONS VEGETABLE OIL

ONE 4-INCH CINNAMON STICK

3 GREEN CARDAMOM PODS, CRUSHED

½ TEASPOON FENNEL SEEDS, CRUSHED

½ TEASPOON CUMIN SEEDS, CRUSHED

2 SMALL RED ONIONS, ROUGHLY CHOPPED

2 FRESH RED OR GREEN CHILES, SEEDED AND SLICED LENGTHWISE

1 TABLESPOON GINGER-GARLIC PASTE (PAGE 59)

2 SPRIGS FRESH CURRY LEAVES

3 MEDIUM TOMATOES, CUT IN HALF

1½ POUNDS BONE-IN LAMB SHOULDER, CUT INTO 1½-INCH CUBES

1 TABLESPOON GROUND CORIANDER

2 MEDIUM RED POTATOES, PEELED AND CUT IN HALF

2 TABLESPOONS KORMA MASALA (PAGE 48 OR STORE-BOUGHT)

1 TEASPOON SALT, OR TO TASTE

¼ CUP PLAIN YOGURT

1. Heat the oil in a large heavy pot or Dutch oven over medium heat. Add the cinnamon, cardamom pods, fennel, cumin, onions, chiles, ginger-garlic paste, and curry leaves. Cook, stirring, until the onions are soft and fragrant, about 10 minutes.

2. Add the tomatoes, lamb, and coriander and give it a good stir. Add 1 cup water, cover the pot, and bring to a boil over medium heat. Add the potatoes and korma masala and stir well. Reduce the heat to low and simmer, stirring occasionally, until the meat is tender, about 40 minutes. Ground coriander tends to make the curry thick, so you may add ½ cup water to the pot to thin it.

3. Season with salt to taste. Add the yogurt and stir until blended. Raise the heat to medium and bring to a gentle boil without stirring, about 2 minutes. Remove from the heat and serve hot.

Braised Pork in Caramelized Soy Sauce

I grew up on this rustic dish. I distinctly remember the fragrance of ginger and tomatoes sizzling in the pan with pieces of pork in sweet soy sauce. It would come out looking heavenly, reddish brown with an aroma that would get my mouth watering. Even now, every time I prepare this dish, my kids dash downstairs, asking "When's dinner, Mom?" just as I did when I was little. Serve with Perfect Jasmine Rice (page 176) and Stir-Fried Bean Sprouts with White Pepper (page 113). SERVES 4

3 TABLESPOONS VEGETABLE OIL

ONE 2-INCH PIECE FRESH GINGER, PEELED AND CUT INTO THICK STRIPS

5 GARLIC CLOVES, CHOPPED

1 FRESH RED CHILE, SEEDED AND THINLY SLICED

2 SPRIGS FRESH CURRY LEAVES

ONE 2-INCH CINNAMON STICK

2 STAR ANISE

1 LARGE RED ONION, CUT INTO THICK RINGS

2 RIPE TOMATOES, QUARTERED

1 ½ POUNDS BONELESS PORK SHOULDER, CUT INTO 1-INCH CUBES

2 TABLESPOONS SOY SAUCE

3 TABLESPOONS SWEET SOY SAUCE

¼ TEASPOON FRESHLY GROUND WHITE PEPPER

PINCH OF SALT

1. Heat the oil in a saucepan over medium heat. When the oil is hot, add the ginger, garlic, chile, curry leaves, cinnamon, star anise, and half of the onion. Cook, stirring, until the ginger and onion rings turn light brown and smell fragrant, about 7 minutes.

2. Add the tomatoes and cook, stirring, for 5 minutes. Add the pork and mix well to coat with the spices. Turn the heat to low, cover, and simmer, stirring occasionally, for 35 minutes, until the pork is very soft.

3. Add the remaining onion, the soy sauce, sweet soy sauce, pepper, and salt. Raise the heat to medium, mix well, and cook for 5 minutes, until the sauce has thickened. Remove from the heat and serve hot.

Thai Green Pork Curry

The green chile and cilantro used in this recipe give the curry a green color but, more important, impart their distinct flavors. When these spices mingle with the coconut milk and other aromatics in the pot, the real essence of green curry flavor is created. This is a classic Thai curry, and once you get the curry right, it does not matter what kind of meat you put into it—the curry will always exude a citruslike fragrance and taste exquisite. Serve with Perfect Jasmine Rice (page 176). SERVES 4

Clockwise from left: Thai Green Pork Curry, Papaya and Prawn Salad (page 89), and Stir-Fried Chicken with Cashews (page 124)

2½ TABLESPOONS CANOLA OR PEANUT OIL

¼ CUP THAI GREEN CURRY PASTE (PAGE 57 OR STORE-BOUGHT)

1 FRESH RED CHILE, SEEDED AND THINLY SLICED

¼ TEASPOON FRESHLY GROUND BLACK PEPPER

¼ CUP FIRMLY PACKED FRESH KAFFIR LIME LEAVES, STEMMED

1 POUND BONELESS PORK SHOULDER, CUT INTO 1-INCH CUBES

2 MEDIUM RED POTATOES, PEELED AND QUARTERED

ONE 14-OUNCE CAN COCONUT MILK (PAGE 26)

2 TEASPOONS FISH SAUCE, OR TO TASTE

1½ TO 2 TABLESPOONS PALM SUGAR SYRUP (PAGE 27) OR BROWN SUGAR

PINCH OF SALT

⅓ CUP FIRMLY PACKED FRESH ASIAN SWEET BASIL

1. Heat the oil in a large pot over medium heat. When the oil is hot, add the curry paste, chile, pepper, and lime leaves. Cook, stirring constantly, until aromatic and the oils separate from the spice paste, about 5 minutes.

2. Add the pork and potatoes and mix well. Cover, turn the heat to low, and simmer, stirring occasionally, for 25 minutes, or until the potatoes and pork are tender.

3. Add the coconut milk and cook over medium heat for 5 minutes. Add the fish sauce, palm sugar syrup, and salt. Stir and taste, adding more fish sauce to taste. Stir in the basil and heat through for 30 seconds. Remove from the heat and serve hot.

Malaysia Market Noodles (page 190); opposite, Spiced Salmon with Fennel and Tomato (page 169)

Coconut
Spareribs
(page 76)

Pineapple,
Jicama,
and Green
Mango with
Tamarind
Sauce
(page 98)

Lemon Pepper Wings (page 72); opposite, Peppered Beef Salad (page 90)

Pineapple Pickle (page 197), Perfect Jasmine Rice (page 176), and Basil Chicken (page 121)

Thai Shrimp and Pineapple Curry (page 157)

Steamed Snapper with Tamarind-Ginger Sauce (page 164)

Basil Fried Rice (page 183); opposite, Penang-style Vegetable Pickle (page 195)

Black Rice
Pudding
(page 213);
opposite,
Cinnamon
Chocolate
Cake
(page 210)

Seafood

Thai Shrimp and Pineapple Curry

✦

Southeast Asian–Style Seafood Bouillabaisse

✦

Scallop and Vegetable Stir-Fry

✦

Shrimp in Sweet-Sour Sauce

✦

Garlic Prawns

✦

Masala Shrimp with Fragrant Curry Leaves

✦

Steamed Snapper with Tamarind-Ginger Sauce

✦

Halibut Braised in Coconut Sambal

✦

Broiled Cod in Chile-Tamarind Sauce

✦

Salmon with Ginger Butter

✦

Spiced Salmon with Fennel and Tomato

I had eagerly anticipated my first trip to Pulau Aur, Malaysia's most distant island, some 90 nautical miles deep into the South China Sea, when I was working on a documentary project for a public relations firm. After a long drive from Kuala Lumpur, across the main mountain range and through little *kampungs,* or villages, lining the country road, my friends and I arrived at Mersing, a sleepy hollow port of sorts that bustles with tourists headed for Pulau Aur on weekends.

There we met Dr. Linus, an old friend of my father's, who operated a bed-and-breakfast in addition to a clinic. I was amused to hear stories of how, on occasion, he would receive his doctor's fee in the form of freshly caught fish or other local produce by the patients he treats. But what I really remember is his great-tasting pepper crab soup, which he prepared like a master chef.

After eating to our hearts' content, we waited at the jetty for our boat. Soon our friendly *tekong,* or boatman, packed us in and we were off like a blur on a small fishing boat. From the muddy water at the *sungai,* or river mouth, we hit the open blue sea.

Four hours later, the sight of Pulau Aur's hazy outline, bluish green on the horizon, made me tingle. As I was soaking in the excitement, our captain signaled his mates to prepare the jig for fishing. "Sister, can we stop a while to catch dinner?" he requested politely.

For the life of me, I had never seen anything like it. These guys had a long fishing line with scores of tiny hooks that ended with a jade-green luminous stud, the sort used in watches to show time at night. They threw their line without any bait and within minutes yanked out ten to fifteen one-foot-long yellowjacks. After repeating this a couple of times, they had two buckets full of fish.

Finally, we swung into the waters of Pulau Aur, protected by two forested outcrops. Moving closer to shore, we could see the shadow of our boat on rocks 40 feet below in the crystal-clear water, where live coral fringed the island.

We were thrilled to settle into very basic A-frame wooden chalets thatched with dried coconut leaves. Warm greetings ensued, and the *machik*, grandlady of the chalets and caretaker, together with her teenage daughters, began to prepare dinner. From her garden patch, she collected bunches of tiny *terung*, which are eggplants the size of plums, and the most amazing looking *chili padi* I have ever seen—fiery bird's-eye chiles no bigger than the size of a peanut and blackish red in color. She pounded these with slices of fresh young mango and shrimp paste to make the island's signature sambal, to be eaten with fried fish. There were also clams and mussels and the local *ulams*, or raw herbs the islanders eat as salad. The seafood was so unabashedly fresh that it had a tinge of salinity in every bite.

Pulau Aur will always be etched in my mind as the heavenly island where I first fell in love with fresh seafood cooked the way islanders have learned to preserve its delicate textures and taste.

Though we don't have a chance to catch our own fish off an island paradise too often, when you shop for seafood, you should look for what is freshest in the market. If you want a whole fish, for instance, take a look at the eyes. They should be clear and bright, not sunken or cloudy. The flesh should be firm when pressed with your finger. Fresh fish and seafood always have a pleasant aroma.

When buying hard-shell clams, mussels, or oysters, choose ones with tightly closed shells. An open or broken shell means the shellfish is dead and should not be eaten. At home I always place fresh clams in a bucket of cold water with some sea salt and cornmeal. This helps the clams to spit out any sand. Mussels should be scrubbed and debearded before cooking. When buying shucked oysters, look for ones packed in their own liquid, which should be clear. Scallops—either sea scallops, which are 2 inches in diameter, or bay scallops, which are ½ to 1 inch in diameter—are sold in supermarkets already shucked and cleaned. Look for ones that are ivory in color and smell fresh and sweet.

In Southeast Asia, the word *prawn* is often used interchangeably with the word *shrimp*. Prawns are consumed more than any other crustacean. Choose unshelled prawns that have a shiny firm shell tightly attached to its body. The color should be bright, and the texture firm.

One of the biggest mistakes you can make with seafood is overcooking it. For example, squid rings should be cooked for only 1 to 2 minutes, depending on their thickness.

Salmon should be just warmed through in the center. The longer you cook seafood, the drier and tougher it gets.

I have included some simple-to-prepare Southeast Asian recipes for seafood in this chapter. Recipes such as Thai Shrimp and Pineapple Curry, Southeast Asian–Style Seafood Bouillabaisse, Steamed Snapper with Tamarind-Ginger Sauce, and Spiced Salmon with Fennel and Tomato are among the many I have put together in my kitchen using seafood readily available in Washington. Some recipes have also been gathered from my travels to exotic islands, where seafood is consumed in abundance using fresh ingredients like spices and herbs. I hope you'll give these recipes a try, using your favorite seafood, preferably what's locally available.

Thai Shrimp and Pineapple Curry

Even people who claim to dislike curry always come back for a second helping after sampling this dish. The pairing of fruit and shrimp is a mouthwatering combination. The grapes and pineapple bring out the fruity flavors of the shrimp curry, making it neither too spicy nor too mild, just remarkably exotic. Serve with Perfect Jasmine Rice (page 176) and Green Papaya Salad (page 94). SERVES 4

½ CUP COCONUT CREAM (PAGE 26)

2 TABLESPOONS CILANTRO-GARLIC PASTE (PAGE 60)

2 TABLESPOONS THAI RED CURRY PASTE (PAGE 56 OR STORE-BOUGHT)

¼ TEASPOON GROUND CUMIN

¼ TEASPOON GROUND CORIANDER

1 CUP CANNED COCONUT MILK (PAGE 26)

6 FRESH KAFFIR LIME LEAVES, STEMMED AND TORN

1 TO 1½ TABLESPOONS PALM SUGAR SYRUP (PAGE 27) OR BROWN SUGAR

2 TABLESPOONS FISH SAUCE

½ TEASPOON SALT

8 OUNCES FIRM TOFU, DRAINED AND CUT INTO ½-INCH CUBES

½ CUP SEEDLESS RED GRAPES, HALVED

½ CUP PEELED, CORED, AND CUBED FRESH PINEAPPLE

12 OUNCES LARGE SHRIMP, PEELED AND DEVEINED

8 FRESH RED CHILES, THINLY SLICED

1 CUP FRESH ASIAN SWEET BASIL LEAVES

1. Put the coconut cream, cilantro-garlic paste, red curry paste, cumin, and coriander in a wok or large sauté pan over medium heat and cook until the oil starts to separate from the cream and appears on the top, about 10 minutes.

2. Gradually pour in the coconut milk, add the lime leaves, and bring just to a boil.

3. In a small bowl, combine the palm sugar syrup, fish sauce, and salt. Mix thoroughly.

4. Reduce the heat to low, add the fish sauce mixture, and stir well to combine. Simmer for 5 minutes. Add the tofu, grapes, pineapple, and shrimp and cook until the shrimp turn bright orange and feel slightly firm, about 2 minutes. Stir in the chiles and basil leaves and cook for another minute. Remove from the heat and serve hot.

Southeast Asian–Style Seafood Bouillabaisse

This is my Southeast Asian version of the famous French bouillabaisse. After returning from Seattle's Pike Place Market one day with a basketful of too much fresh seafood—clams, mussels, shrimp, scallops, and salmon—I didn't have the heart to freeze any of it. Instead, I combined three quintessentially Southeast Asian basics—spices, coconut milk, and curry leaves—with the seafood, transforming the bouillabaisse into an aromatic, delicate, and sensational dish. This dish is best served with bread or over angel hair pasta for a Mediterranean-Asian twist. SERVES 4

4 TO 6 DRIED RED CHILES, TO TASTE, CHOPPED

1 TEASPOON CORIANDER SEEDS

1 TEASPOON CUMIN SEEDS

6 BLACK PEPPERCORNS

1 TABLESPOON PLUS 1 TEASPOON GINGER-GARLIC PASTE (PAGE 59)

2 TABLESPOONS SWEET SOY SAUCE

1 TEASPOON DISTILLED WHITE VINEGAR

¼ CUP PLUS 1 TABLESPOON EXTRA VIRGIN OLIVE OIL

2 SPRIGS FRESH CURRY LEAVES

½ MEDIUM YELLOW ONION, CHOPPED

1 CUP CANNED COCONUT CREAM (PAGE 26)

½ TEASPOON GROUND TURMERIC

8 OUNCES LARGE SHRIMP, PEELED AND DEVEINED

8 OUNCES LARGE SCALLOPS, CUT IN HALF HORIZONTALLY

8 OUNCES CLAMS, SCRUBBED

8 OUNCES MUSSELS, SCRUBBED AND DEBEARDED

8 OUNCES SKINLESS SALMON FILLET

1 TEASPOON UNSALTED BUTTER

1 TEASPOON SALT, OR TO TASTE

½ CUP CHOPPED FRESH CILANTRO LEAVES

1. Soak the dried chiles in ½ cup hot water until soft, about 15 minutes. Drain well.

2. Combine the chiles, coriander, cumin, peppercorns, ginger-garlic paste, sweet soy sauce, and vinegar in a food processor. Cover and blend to a coarse paste. Set the spice paste aside.

3. Heat the olive oil in a deep skillet over medium heat. Add the curry leaves and onion, and cook, stirring, until the onion is soft and translucent, about 5 minutes.

Add the spice paste and cook until aromatic, reddish brown in color, and the oils separate on the surface, 8 to 10 minutes.

4. Add the coconut cream, 1 cup water, and the turmeric and bring to a boil. Add the shrimp, scallops, clams, mussels, and salmon. Cover and simmer until the clams and mussels open, 3 to 4 minutes. Discard any clams and mussels that remain closed.

5. Add the butter and salt and mix well. Garnish with fresh cilantro and serve immediately.

Scallop and Vegetable Stir-Fry

The Malaysian culinary way of life is unique in that if you cannot go to the market, the market comes to you. It is common to be graced with a morning visit from the friendly fishmonger, who sells his provisions from a van. This purveyor of seafood often hoots his call to housewives, who make a beeline to purchase the freshest seafood, as well as to gossip and exchange recipes. Their purchases, more often than not, are recorded in a little account book and the bill settled at the end of the month. This simple but tasty scallop and vegetable stir-fry is a recipe from one of our neighbors. Serve it with Perfect Jasmine Rice (page 176). SERVES 4

2 TABLESPOONS CANOLA OR PEANUT OIL	8 OUNCES BABY CORN, CUT IN HALF
2 GARLIC CLOVES, MINCED	⅓ CUP BEAN SPROUTS
1 SMALL WHITE ONION, FINELY SLICED	¼ CUP SOY SAUCE
12 OUNCES MEDIUM SCALLOPS, CUT IN HALF HORIZONTALLY	3 TABLESPOONS OYSTER SAUCE
1½ CUPS BROCCOLI FLORETS	2 TABLESPOONS FRIED SHALLOTS (PAGE 204; OPTIONAL) FOR GARNISH
12 OUNCES SHIITAKE MUSHROOMS, STEMMED AND CUT INTO ½-INCH PIECES	¼ CUP FRESH CILANTRO LEAVES
1 SMALL CARROT, SLICED ON THE DIAGONAL	

1. Heat a wok or large nonstick sauté pan over medium heat for 40 seconds and then add the oil around the perimeter of the wok so that it coats the sides and bottom. When the surface shimmers slightly, after about 30 seconds, add the garlic and onion and cook, stirring, until golden brown, about 3 minutes. Immediately toss in the scallops and cook, pressing the scallops against the side of the hot wok to sear them, for 1 minute, until light brown.

2. Add the broccoli, mushrooms, carrot, baby corn, and bean sprouts and cook, stirring, for 3 minutes, until the vegetables are half cooked. Add the soy sauce and oyster sauce and cook, stirring, for 2 minutes.

3. Remove from the heat and transfer to a serving dish. Add the fried shallots and cilantro and serve immediately.

Shrimp in Sweet-Sour Sauce A lovely combination of tropical Asian flavors, this dish exudes a perfect balance of sweet and sour. You may replace the sauce in this recipe with 1 cup Sweet-Sour Sauce (page 65) for a slightly different flavor; both versions are fantastic. The Sriracha chile sauce I use here is a tart chile sauce sold at all Asian supermarkets. I have taught this recipe in many cooking classes, and over the years it has become my students' favorite sweet-sour shrimp dish. SERVES 4

½ CUP KETCHUP

¼ CUP PLUS 2 TABLESPOONS DISTILLED WHITE VINEGAR

¼ CUP SUGAR

2 TO 2½ TABLESPOONS SRIRACHA CHILE SAUCE, TO TASTE

¼ CUP VEGETABLE OIL

5 GARLIC CLOVES, CHOPPED

ONE 4-INCH PIECE FRESH GINGER, PEELED AND FINELY SLICED

2 RED BELL PEPPERS, DICED

1 POUND LARGE SHRIMP, PEELED AND DEVEINED

1 TABLESPOON CORNSTARCH MIXED WITH 1 TABLESPOON WATER

2 TABLESPOONS FISH SAUCE

5 SCALLIONS, BOTH WHITE AND GREEN PARTS, CHOPPED

1. Combine the ketchup, vinegar, sugar, and chile sauce in a bowl and mix well. Set the sauce aside.

2. Heat a wok or large nonstick sauté pan over medium heat for 40 seconds and then add the oil around the perimeter of the wok so that it coats the sides and bottom. When the surface shimmers slightly, after about 30 seconds, add the garlic and ginger and cook, stirring constantly, until the garlic appears golden, about 2 minutes. Toss in the red bell peppers, raise the heat to high, and cook, stirring, for 2 minutes. Add the shrimp and cook, stirring constantly, until bright orange, 4 minutes.

3. Pour in the sauce and mix well to coat. Allow the sauce to cook for 1 minute and then add the cornstarch mixture to thicken. Season with the fish sauce. Toss in the scallions and mix well. Remove from the heat and serve immediately.

Garlic Prawns The island of Phuket, Thailand, just an hour across the Andaman Sea from Malaysia, is undoubtedly my favorite destination on my visits home. Every year in May, Phuket celebrates its Seafood Festival to attract visitors during the rainy season. You'll find quite a few open-air seafood restaurants displaying the catch of the day over crushed ice laid out on buffet tables. In the evenings, these restaurants set up large woks on the street and cook up a variety of prawn dishes to attract passersby. I simply adore this Phuket-style dish; the aromatic flavors of the basil come alive, pleasantly intense with a little hint of sweetness from the sweet soy sauce. Serve this dish with Perfect Jasmine Rice (page 176) and Green Apple and Mango Salad (page 92). SERVES 4

3 TABLESPOONS CANOLA OR PEANUT OIL

10 GARLIC CLOVES, MINCED

1 POUND MEDIUM PRAWNS OR JUMBO SHRIMP, PEELED AND DEVEINED

½ TEASPOON WHITE PEPPERCORNS, CRUSHED

2 TABLESPOONS OYSTER SAUCE

1 TABLESPOON SWEET SOY SAUCE

3 SCALLIONS, BOTH WHITE AND GREEN PARTS, CHOPPED

1 CUP FRESH ASIAN SWEET BASIL LEAVES, COARSELY CHOPPED

1. Heat a wok or large nonstick sauté pan over medium heat for 40 seconds and then add the oil around the perimeter of the wok so that it coats the sides and bottom. When the surface shimmers slightly, after about 30 seconds, add the garlic and cook, stirring, for 2 minutes, until golden.

2. Add the prawns and cook, stirring, until bright orange, 4 minutes. If you have too much liquid in the wok, which comes naturally as the prawns cook, raise the heat to high to evaporate the liquid.

3. Add the white pepper, oyster sauce, sweet soy sauce, and scallions and cook, stirring, for 2 minutes. Toss in the basil leaves and cook until wilted, 1 minute. Remove from the heat, transfer to a serving platter, and serve immediately.

Masala Shrimp with Fragrant Curry Leaves

In the summer, I always have a large bowl of fresh, juicy tomatoes from the garden in my kitchen. This is when I enjoy making this rustic dish, redolent of sweet roasted tomatoes. When preparing this recipe, make sure the onions and tomatoes are cooked down perfectly before adding the chile. The moistness of the tomatoes will absorb the chile and deliver a lovely mélange of sweet and hot flavors. Serve this dish with Mild Coconut Curry with Tomatoes (page 116) and a hot plate of Basmati Rice (page 177) for a classic Malaysian Indian home-cooked dinner. SERVES 4

¼ CUP CANOLA OR PEANUT OIL

1 SMALL YELLOW ONION, MINCED

2 SPRIGS FRESH CURRY LEAVES

1 TOMATO, QUARTERED

½ TEASPOON GROUND TURMERIC

1 TEASPOON PURE CHILE POWDER (PAGE 17) OR CAYENNE

1 POUND LARGE SHRIMP, PEELED AND DEVEINED

1 TEASPOON SALT, OR TO TASTE

1. Heat a wok or large nonstick sauté pan over medium heat for 40 seconds and then add the oil around the perimeter of the wok so that it coats the sides and bottom. When the surface shimmers slightly, after about 30 seconds, add the onion, curry leaves, and tomato. Cook until the onion and tomato are soft and fragrant, about 12 minutes.

2. Add the turmeric and chile powder, stir, and cook for 2 to 3 minutes. Add the shrimp and 2 tablespoons water. Cook the shrimp until they are pink and slightly firm, about 3 minutes. Season with salt, stir well, and remove from the heat. Transfer to a serving platter and serve immediately.

Steamed Snapper with Tamarind-Ginger Sauce

The delicate taste of snapper is enhanced in this dish by a tangy tamarind sauce and the citrusy aroma of ginger. The whole fish is steamed and then finished with a drizzle of hot oil that will mingle with the sauce to create a sizzle without leaving the fish greasy. The results are incredible. Any other light-tasting fish such as true cod, mahimahi, halibut, trout, or sea bass also works well here, including fish fillets if you prefer them.

In this recipe, I have used a 10-inch round bamboo steamer to steam the fish, although you may use a regular steamer. I prefer the bamboo steamer as it has a tight lid and the insert basket fits perfectly onto a wok to trap the steam. During steaming, excess water is absorbed by the bamboo instead of falling directly on the fish, as in the case of a metal steamer. Bamboo steamers are inexpensive, and you'll find them at most Asian supermarkets or on the Internet.

Serve with Stir-Fried Bean Sprouts with White Pepper (page 113) or Stir-Fried Bok Choy and Shiitake Mushrooms with Garlic (page 117) if desired.

SERVES 2 TO 4

ONE 5-INCH PIECE FRESH GALANGAL, PEELED AND THINLY SLICED

ONE 5-INCH PIECE FRESH GINGER, PEELED AND THINLY SLICED

ONE 1½-POUND WHOLE SNAPPER, SCALED AND CLEANED

½ SMALL HEAD GREEN CABBAGE, ROUGHLY CHOPPED

3 FRESH RED CHILES, THINLY SLICED

3 TABLESPOONS FISH SAUCE, OR TO TASTE

3 TABLESPOONS TAMARIND LIQUID (PAGE 35)

3 TABLESPOONS PALM SUGAR SYRUP (PAGE 27) OR BROWN SUGAR

3 TABLESPOONS FRESH LIME JUICE

3 TABLESPOONS RICE WINE

¼ CUP COARSELY CHOPPED FRESH CILANTRO LEAVES

3 TABLESPOONS PEANUT OIL

---

1. Fill half of a wok with water so the water line is just below the bottom of the bamboo steamer. Add half of the sliced galangal and ginger to the water. Bring the water to a boil over medium heat.

2. Meanwhile, pat the fish dry with paper towels. With a sharp knife, make 3 diagonal slashes on each side of the fish; set aside.

3. Arrange the cabbage evenly in the steamer basket. The cabbage will prevent the fish from sticking to the bamboo. Place the fish on top of the cabbage. Arrange the chiles and the remaining galangal and ginger over the fish. Set the steamer basket on the wok. Cover the basket and steam for 15 minutes. To check the fish, insert the tip of a knife into the center of the fish. When cooked, the flesh will be white.

4. While the fish is steaming, make the sauce by combining the fish sauce, tamarind liquid, palm sugar syrup, and lime juice in a small pan. Bring to a boil over medium heat. Taste and add more fish sauce if needed. Turn off the heat, add the rice wine, and mix well. Set aside.

5. Carefully remove the steamer lid to avoid scalding yourself with the steam. With a flat spatula, gently lift the fish, including the chiles, ginger, and galangal, and transfer to a serving platter. Sprinkle with cilantro. Now pour the seasoning sauce over the fish.

6. Heat the oil in a small pan until it begins to smoke. Remove from the heat and carefully drizzle the hot oil over the fish. Serve immediately.

Halibut Braised in Coconut Sambal

Here is a mild sambal recipe to accentuate the sweet flavor of halibut. In Malaysia, this is a common home-cooked dish, using locally available fresh fish. I love the taste of Pacific halibut whenever it is in season, but you may substitute a similar firm white fish. Instead of cooking this on the stovetop, you may also bake the fish wrapped in banana leaves in the oven for 20 minutes. The leaves will retain the sambal flavors, imparting their own subtle aroma to the fish. Remember to drizzle some sambal over hot rice—it is addictive. SERVES 4

5 GARLIC CLOVES

4 TO 6 FRESH RED CHILES, TO TASTE, ROUGHLY CHOPPED

2 SMALL SHALLOTS, CHOPPED

1 TABLESPOON SHRIMP PASTE, TOASTED (PAGE 34)

¼ CUP CANOLA OR PEANUT OIL

1 CUP CANNED COCONUT MILK (PAGE 26)

1 TABLESPOON SUGAR

¼ TEASPOON SALT, OR TO TASTE

1½ POUNDS BONE-IN HALIBUT STEAK (1 INCH THICK), CUT INTO 4-INCH PIECES

1. Combine the garlic, chiles, shallots, and shrimp paste in a food processor. Grind into a smooth paste, adding a little water if necessary to keep the blades moving.

2. Heat the oil in a large saucepan pan over medium heat. Carefully add the spice paste and cook, stirring occasionally, for 7 minutes. Gradually add the coconut milk, stirring it into the spice paste, then add the sugar and salt and simmer for 10 minutes, or until the oils come to the surface.

3. Add the fish and cook until cooked through, about 10 minutes. Taste, adding more salt if needed. Remove from the heat and serve hot.

Cook's Tip *To save time, I sometimes cook the coconut sambal in advance and freeze it in freezer bags. To get dinner ready, I simply reheat the sambal with the catch of the day.*

Broiled Cod in Chile-Tamarind Sauce

This is my healthy version of the Thai-style crispy fried fish with chile-tamarind sauce. The cod is remarkably light yet bursting with the cuisine's characteristic flavor combination of sweet, spicy, salty, and sour. SERVES 4

1 POUND SKINLESS COD FILLET

1 TABLESPOON CANOLA OR PEANUT OIL

2 GARLIC CLOVES, MINCED

2 FRESH RED CHILES, MINCED

2 SMALL SHALLOTS, CHOPPED

3 TABLESPOONS FISH SAUCE

3 TABLESPOONS TAMARIND LIQUID (PAGE 35)

3 TABLESPOONS PALM SUGAR SYRUP (PAGE 27) OR BROWN SUGAR

1. Preheat the broiler. Place the fish on a baking sheet and drizzle with the oil. Carefully place the baking sheet on the top rack under the broiler and broil for 10 minutes, or until light golden and cooked through.

2. Meanwhile, combine the garlic, chiles, shallots, fish sauce, tamarind liquid, and palm sugar syrup in a small pan. Bring to a boil over medium heat, then reduce the heat to low and simmer for 5 to 7 minutes.

3. Carefully remove the fish from the broiler and transfer to a serving platter. Pour the sauce over the fish. Serve immediately.

Salmon with Ginger Butter

My children love the teriyaki salmon from the mom-and-pop restaurant near our home. Every now and then, they coax me into buying it as a take-out snack. Their yearning for teriyaki salmon inspired me to create this dish, which contrasts the buttery-soft texture of salmon with subtle hints of fresh ginger, shallots, and scallions with a taste that is similar to teriyaki. The ingredients are effortless to prepare, yet they create magic in the pan. SERVES 4

1 POUND SKINLESS SALMON FILLET

1 TABLESPOON EXTRA VIRGIN OLIVE OIL

2 TABLESPOONS BUTTER

ONE 3-INCH PIECE FRESH GINGER, PEELED AND CUT INTO LONG, THIN MATCHSTICKS

1 SMALL SHALLOT, THINLY SLICED

2 SCALLIONS, BOTH WHITE AND GREEN PARTS, CHOPPED

½ CUP CHICKEN BROTH

1 TABLESPOON OYSTER SAUCE

1 TEASPOON SOY SAUCE, OR TO TASTE

1. Pat the fish dry with paper towels. Cut the fish into 4 pieces. Set aside.

2. Heat the olive oil and butter in a skillet over medium heat. Add the ginger and shallot and cook until light brown in color, about 5 minutes.

3. Add the scallions, chicken broth, oyster sauce, and soy sauce. Bring just to a boil. Taste and add more soy sauce if needed for saltiness. Add the fish pieces and cook for 5 minutes on each side, until most of the liquid is absorbed into the fish and the fish is warm in the center.

4. Transfer the fish to a serving platter, top with the cooked ginger, shallots, and scallions, and serve immediately.

Spiced Salmon with Fennel and Tomato

I love the taste of wild salmon, by far the most popular fish in Seattle. In this dish, the combination of delicate, sweet fennel and coriander perfectly complements the salmon. I make this dish very often, as it's quick to prepare, and serve it with Basmati Rice (page 177). SERVES 4

4 SALMON STEAKS (EACH ABOUT 6 TO 8 OUNCES AND 1 INCH THICK)

1 ¼ TEASPOONS SALT, OR TO TASTE

¼ TEASPOON GROUND TURMERIC

3 TABLESPOONS EXTRA VIRGIN OLIVE OIL

½ SMALL RED ONION, MINCED

6 GARLIC CLOVES, MINCED

2 LARGE TOMATOES, CHOPPED

1 TABLESPOON GROUND FENNEL

1 TEASPOON GROUND CORIANDER

1. Preheat the oven to 350°F. Pat the fish steaks dry with paper towels. Rub the fish on both sides with ¼ teaspoon of the salt and the turmeric. Place the fish steaks on a baking sheet and set aside.

2. Heat the oil in a medium saucepan over medium heat. Add the onion and cook until soft and light brown, about 10 minutes.

3. Add the garlic, tomatoes, fennel, coriander, and remaining teaspoon of salt. Stir and cook until the tomatoes break down, about 3 minutes. You may add a little water to the pan if necessary to prevent the spices from sticking. Taste and add more salt if needed. Remove from the heat.

4. Spoon the cooked tomato mixture over the fish steaks and bake for 15 minutes, until the fish is firm on the outside and warmed through in the center. Serve immediately.

Kaffir limes

Rice and Rice Noodles

Perfect Jasmine Rice

✦

Basmati Rice

✦

Pine Nut and Orange Pilaf

✦

Saffron Pilaf

✦

Cardamom Butter Rice with Sultanas

✦

Fried Rice with Pork, Sausage, and Shiitakes

✦

Basil Fried Rice

✦

Fragrant Herb Rice

✦

Indonesian Sambal Rice with Shrimp

✦

Fresh Rice Noodles with Seafood and Basil

✦

Pad Thai with Chicken

✦

Malaysia Market Noodles

To me as an Asian, rice is not just another grain; it is a staple that touches nearly every aspect of my life. As a child, the first solid food to touch my taste buds after weaning was rice porridge. Rice is a part of everyday life, the fabric upon which much of Asian history is written, the thread that binds communities. It flows through the colorful traditions and literally becomes one with culture—it is the lifeblood of every Asian.

Rice fields, flat and terraced, are seen throughout Southeast Asia. The area from Chiang Rai in the northern plains of Thailand through the flat northern region of Kedah in Malaysia to Bali in the South is dubbed the rice bowl of the nation, and the grain is grown here on a large scale. Although today modern machinery can be seen on these stretches of emerald-green fields, every so often one catches a glimpse of traditional farming methods. For the farmer set in his ways, it is rise and shine at the crack of dawn. With the sky still in its slumber and the morning rays creeping in, the farmer prepares his faithful buffalo for the task of plowing the muddy, waterlogged field. Using a wooden plow, he harvests the field to feed the nation and the world.

I always keep several types of rice in a variety of containers, which I keep full, a practice many Asian cultures still believe brings good luck. Whether steamed or fried, in noodles, cakes, or porridge, rice is the foundation of almost every meal I make at home. For me, the best way to enjoy rice is with my fingers, which is an intimate way of connecting with food. In my rice cooking classes, I always share the proper way to eat rice with your fingers. The proper method begins with a thorough hand washing of course, then, using only the right hand, food is picked up with the lower halves of the fingers, which mix the rice and form it into a neat little mound. The little rice mound is then picked up and pushed into the mouth with the thumb. The center of the palm is always dry.

There are endless ways to celebrate rice. It is a Malaysian tradition to bless newlywed couples by throwing turmeric-colored rice on them as they complete their vows. It signifies fertility and a smooth journey through married life. In the month of April, Malaysian Indians celebrate Tai Pongal, a festival that gives thanks to God for a year of bountiful harvest. Ladies in bright attire gather in the temple courtyard early in the morning, carrying steel pots. Chanting prayers, they light a wood fire that faces the sunrise. They cook rice, brown sugar, and milk in a large pot, allowing it to boil over on the east side, which signals the flow of good luck and fortune in the coming year. The cooked rice is then placed on a banana leaf and offered to God.

Selecting Rice There are journals and articles on the Internet that prove brown rice to be healthier, with more fiber than white rice. While this is true, most Southeast Asians consume white rice instead of brown. Brown rice is chewy and has a nutty texture that does not complement robust curries, powerful sambals, or spicy stir-fried dishes. White rice is smooth, fragrant, and tender and has great absorbing qualities. In the United States, you can find jasmine and basmati rice at larger supermarkets, gourmet stores, and Asian markets. Other varieties of rice, too, are sold at Southeast Asian markets: black sticky rice, used mainly for desserts; white sticky rice, used for desserts, a velvety breakfast porridge, and served with northern Thai cuisine; and finally the red rice from Bali or Thailand, which is nutty and wholesome, a good substitute for brown rice.

Southeast Asians are passionate about their white rice and know that an entire meal can be ruined by flawed rice. As a rule of thumb, if you are serving a dish that has Chinese influences (like fish, soy, or oyster sauce and fresh spices), serve it with white jasmine rice. If the dish has Indian influences—a pilaf, for example, or a curry made with various masalas, aromatics, and dry spices—use basmati. One student in my cooking class commented, "You cannot use jasmine when the dish belongs to basmati."

Jasmine rice is long grained and fragrant, with a natural jasmine scent. Sometimes bags are labeled *new crop*, which means the rice is sold right after harvesting. Should you purchase a bag marked *new crop*, you will need less water when cooking the rice, as explained in my rice recipe pages. The bags that are not marked *new crop* hold rice stored for six months or more after harvesting, making it a little drier and requiring more water for cooking. After cooking, the grains are tender and hold together loosely with a heavenly scent.

Basmati, which translates as "queen of fragrance," is long-grain rice that grows in the foothills of the Himalayan Mountains. This rice is famous for its scent and delicate flavor. The grains of basmati rice are long and narrow, and they grow even longer when cooked. They stay firm and separated and are not sticky after cooking. Basmati is available as either white rice or brown rice. If you are using brown rice, know that it requires more water and longer cooking time.

Fresh rice noodles are made of water and rice flour. The advantage of freshly made rice noodles is that they soak up the sauces quickly, making each strand flavorful. You can find fresh rice noodles in the refrigerated section of Asian markets. The noodles come in a clear wrapper and are labeled *fresh rice noodles*. Through the plastic you'll see that the noodles are folded white sheets or sometimes precut into ribbons or thin strands. It's best to use fresh rice noodles soon after you buy them, preferably the same day. Do not refrigerate them or the noodles will become hard.

In this chapter, I have also used dried rice noodles, known as *rice stick noodles*. These noodles are flat and come in a variety of thicknesses, in 16-ounce packages. You must always soak dried noodles in hot water until soft before using them. Once soaked, the noodles double in size and a 16-ounce pack is sufficient for 12 or more servings. For convenience, I soak and drain noodles in advance and then put them in an airtight container in the refrigerator. This expedites the cooking of noodle dishes.

Washing Rice My cooking students often ask me whether or not to wash rice. I feel strongly that rice, whether jasmine or basmati, must be washed. This does not mean you are washing away the minerals; washing gets rid of the excess starch and any rice dust. The clearer the water after washing, the longer the rice will keep after it is cooked. I normally wash my rice three times before cooking it. It is best to soak basmati rice for at least half an hour in water prior to cooking if you have time. Each grain will absorb the water, and when you finally lift the cover, the cooked rice will be light and fluffy.

Flavoring Rice You can add flavor to rice by cooking it with spices. Just before cooking rice, add a stick of cinnamon, some cardamom, or a pinch of saffron, turmeric, or paprika. Or go with aromatics such as pandan leaves, lemongrass, ginger, or galangal. You'll find many recipes in this chapter that demonstrate the use of spice with rice. The gentle aroma of the spices mingling with the steamed rice is absolutely great.

Perfect Jasmine Rice

Perfect Jasmine Rice I prepare my rice in a rice cooker since it cooks an amazing amount of rice in a relatively short time. If you don't have a rice cooker, the following recipe is the best way to prepare rice. Cook the water down before you cover the pot; this way you have more control over how much water evaporates, which makes all the difference between mushy and fluffy rice. White jasmine rice is suitable for preparing fried rice and serving with any kind of stir-fry dish, but it should never be used for pilaf. I purchase rice labeled *Thai Jasmine* or *milagrosa* for its high quality and scent, but you may substitute locally grown jasmine rice found at most supermarkets. SERVES 4

2 CUPS JASMINE RICE

1. Wash the rice by gently rubbing it with your fingers in a bowl filled with water. When the water becomes cloudy, drain the water and repeat the process until the water is clear.

2. Put the rice and 3 cups of water in a heavy 4-quart pot and bring to a boil over medium heat without stirring. Let the rice boil until steam holes appear in the rice and the surface looks dry, 5 to 7 minutes. Reduce the heat to low, cover the pot with a tight-fitting lid, and cook for 15 minutes. Remove from the heat and let the rice rest, still covered, for about 5 minutes. Uncover and gently fluff the rice with a fork.

Basmati Rice This dish is my comfort food. It goes well with any curry, but for me a plate of steaming hot basmati rice and some chutney will keep me satiated when I am looking for a simple meal. SERVES 4

2 CUPS WHITE BASMATI RICE

½ TEASPOON SALT

1 TABLESPOON UNSALTED BUTTER

1. Wash the rice by gently rubbing it with your fingers in a bowl filled with water. When the water becomes cloudy, drain the water and repeat the process until the water is clear.

2. Put the rice, 2½ cups water, the salt, and the butter in a heavy 4-quart pot and bring to a boil over medium heat without stirring. Let the rice boil until steam holes appear in the rice and the surface looks dry, 5 to 7 minutes. Reduce the heat to low, cover the pot with a tight-fitting lid, and cook for 20 minutes. Remove from the heat and let the rice rest, still covered, for about 5 minutes. Uncover and gently fluff the rice with a fork.

Pine Nut and Orange Pilaf

Pine nuts are cream-colored nuts that come from dried pinecones. Lightly toasted, they add a sweet, buttery flavor and crunch to this pilaf. You can always substitute slivered almonds in their place if you wish. I love to serve this pilaf with Merchant's Fried Chicken (page 125). You can make this dish festive for the holidays by substituting dried cranberries for the raisins. SERVES 4 TO 6

3½ CUPS WHITE BASMATI RICE

2 TABLESPOONS UNSALTED BUTTER

4 CLOVES

ONE 1-INCH PIECE FRESH GINGER, PEELED AND THINLY SLICED

3 FRESH BAY LEAVES OR 5 DRIED BAY LEAVES

1½ TEASPOONS DRIED THYME

3 TEASPOONS GRATED FRESH ORANGE ZEST

2 CUPS VEGETABLE BROTH

1 CUP FRESH ORANGE JUICE

1 TEASPOON SALT

2 TABLESPOONS EXTRA VIRGIN OLIVE OIL

1 CUP PINE NUTS

1 CUP RAISINS OR SULTANAS (GOLDEN RAISINS)

½ CUP FRESH CILANTRO LEAVES, ROUGHLY CHOPPED

1. Wash the rice by gently rubbing it with your fingers in a bowl filled with water. When the water becomes cloudy, drain the water and repeat the process until the water is clear. Drain and set the rice aside.

2. Melt the butter in a deep saucepan over low heat. Add the cloves, ginger, bay leaves, thyme, and orange zest. Cook until aromatic, about 3 minutes. Add the rice and cook, stirring, until the grains turn slightly whitish in color and are well coated with the spices, about 7 minutes.

3. Pour in the vegetable broth and orange juice and season with salt. Bring to a boil over medium heat without stirring. Let the rice boil until steam holes appear in the rice and the surface looks dry, about 5 minutes. Reduce the heat to low, cover the pot with a tight-fitting lid, and cook, without stirring, for 20 minutes, or until the broth is fully absorbed and the grains are tender and fluffy.

4. Meanwhile, heat the olive oil in a large saucepan over low heat. Add the pine nuts and cook lightly until golden brown and fragrant, about 4 minutes. Remove

the nuts from the oil using a slotted spoon and drain them on a paper towel. Set aside. Add the raisins to the same pan and cook for 1 minute, until they puff up. Remove from the heat and set aside on the paper towel.

5. Discard the bay leaves and gently fluff the rice with a fork. Fold in the pine nuts, raisins, and cilantro. Serve warm.

Jonker Street in Malacca is home to antique and souvenir shops

Saffron Pilaf When you take this pilaf to the table, it elevates all other dishes you are serving. The rice is first cooked on the stovetop and later covered and baked in the oven. The low heat results in fluffy, loose grains of rice that are golden from saffron. My dad called this "Cleopatra's rice" at home because it makes a rich and grand presentation. SERVES 4 TO 6

3 CUPS WHITE BASMATI RICE	½ TEASPOON SAFFRON THREADS
3 TABLESPOONS UNSALTED BUTTER	1 TEASPOON SALT
1 BAY LEAF	3 TABLESPOONS EXTRA VIRGIN OLIVE OIL
6 GREEN CARDAMOM PODS, CRUSHED	2 TABLESPOONS SLIVERED ALMONDS
ONE 2-INCH CINNAMON STICK	2 TABLESPOONS RAISINS
½ MEDIUM WHITE ONION, MINCED	

1. Preheat the oven to 300°F. Wash the rice by gently rubbing it with your fingers in a bowl filled with water. When the water becomes cloudy, drain the water and repeat the process until the water is clear. Drain and set the rice aside.

2. Melt the butter in a deep ovenproof saucepan over low heat. Add the bay leaf, cardamom, and cinnamon and cook for a few seconds, until fragrant. Add the onion, then raise the heat to medium and cook until translucent, about 5 minutes.

3. Carefully add 3 cups water, the saffron, and the salt. Stir well and bring to a boil. Add the rice, stir, and reduce the heat to medium-low. Let the rice boil gently, until steam holes appear in the rice and the surface looks dry, about 6 minutes.

4. Cover the pot with a tight-fitting lid and transfer it to the oven. Bake until the rice is light and fluffy, about 20 minutes. Carefully remove the pot from the oven, uncover, and fluff the rice with a fork. Cover and set aside.

5. Meanwhile, warm the olive oil in a small sauté pan over low heat. Add the almonds and cook until golden brown and fragrant, about 5 minutes. Remove with a slotted spoon and drain them on a paper towel. Add the raisins to the pan and cook for 1 minute, until they puff up. Set aside on the paper towel.

6. Fluff the rice again and fold in the almonds and raisins. Serve warm.

Cardamom Butter Rice with Sultanas

This rice dish is special to me because it has been in my family for generations. The cardamom-scented butter coats the rice like perfume. Quick and easy to prepare, this buttered rice goes well with fried chicken or fish, Lemon Pepper Wings (page 72), and roast or curried dishes. Taking this flavorful rice to the table with its contrasting colors makes me feel as though I have fed my eyes before my mouth. SERVES 4 TO 6

3½ CUPS WHITE BASMATI RICE

4 TABLESPOONS (½ STICK) UNSALTED BUTTER

1 TABLESPOON GINGER-GARLIC PASTE (PAGE 59)

3 SPRIGS FRESH CURRY LEAVES OR 6 DRIED BAY LEAVES

8 GREEN CARDAMOM PODS, CRUSHED

1½ CUPS FROZEN GREEN PEAS, THAWED

¼ TEASPOON GROUND TURMERIC

1 TEASPOON SALT

3 CUPS VEGETABLE BROTH

¼ CUP SULTANAS (GOLDEN RAISINS)

1. Wash the rice by gently rubbing it with your fingers in a bowl filled with water. When the water becomes cloudy, drain the water and repeat the process until the water is clear. Drain and set the rice aside.

2. Heat the butter in a large saucepan over medium heat. Add the ginger-garlic paste, curry leaves, and cardamom. Sauté until fragrant, about 5 minutes. Add the rice and cook until the grains turn a little whitish in color, about 7 minutes. Add the peas, turmeric, and salt. Cook, stirring, for approximately 4 minutes, until the grains are well coated and the rice appears dry.

3. Add the vegetable broth and stir gently for 30 seconds. Reduce the heat to low, cover the pot with a tight-fitting lid, and cook, without stirring, for 20 minutes, or until all the broth is absorbed and the grains are tender and fluffy.

4. Remove the rice from the heat. Discard the bay leaves and gently fluff the rice with a fork. Fold in the sultanas. Serve warm.

Fried Rice with Pork, Sausage, and Shiitakes

Sweet, chewy *lap cheong*, or Chinese sausage, thinly sliced and lightly charred, adds a wonderful sweet flavor and smokiness to fried rice. You can find this sausage in the refrigerated aisle at Asian markets. This dish is a nourishing way of using up yesterday's rice, and even the kids will love it.

SERVES 2

¼ CUP CANOLA OR PEANUT OIL

4 GARLIC CLOVES, MINCED

ONE 3-INCH PIECE FRESH GINGER, PEELED AND THINLY SLICED

¼ TEASPOON SALT

3 CHINESE SAUSAGE LINKS, THINLY SLICED

5 OUNCES GROUND PORK

8 SHIITAKE MUSHROOM CAPS, SLICED

¼ CUP OYSTER SAUCE

3 TABLESPOONS SOY SAUCE

3 CUPS PERFECT JASMINE RICE (PAGE 176)

4 SCALLIONS, BOTH WHITE AND GREEN PARTS, CHOPPED

1. Heat a wok or large nonstick sauté pan over medium heat for 40 seconds and then add the oil around the perimeter of the wok so that it coats the sides and bottom. When the surface shimmers slightly, after about 30 seconds, add the garlic, ginger, and salt and cook, stirring constantly, until golden brown and fragrant, about 1 minute.

2. Add the sausage and pork and cook, stirring, until the pork is no longer pink, about 6 minutes. Raise the heat to medium-high and add the mushrooms, oyster sauce, and soy sauce. Cook for 1 minute.

3. Add the rice and cook, using a spatula to break up any clumps of rice and mixing the ingredients until well combined, about 4 minutes. Add the scallions, mix well, and remove from the heat. Serve immediately.

Basil Fried Rice Basil leaves are readily available throughout the year at most Asian supermarkets. When shopping, I always pick a bunch, knowing that I am able to use this fragrant herb to make a quick fried rice dish for the family. The fresh basil leaves lend richness with hints of lemon, clove, and anise to the rice when added at the last minute. This dish is packed with flavor and nutrition, combining the tender, juicy shrimp with the herbs. SERVES 2

3 TABLESPOONS CANOLA OR PEANUT OIL

3 GARLIC CLOVES, MINCED

2 SMALL SERRANO CHILES, SEEDED AND CHOPPED

3 SCALLIONS, BOTH WHITE AND GREEN PARTS, CHOPPED

¼ TEASPOON SALT

12 OUNCES LARGE SHRIMP, PEELED AND DEVEINED

3 CUPS PERFECT JASMINE RICE (PAGE 176)

¼ CUP SOY SAUCE

1 TEASPOON FISH SAUCE, OR TO TASTE

½ TEASPOON SUGAR

½ CUP FIRMLY PACKED FRESH ASIAN SWEET BASIL LEAVES, COARSELY CHOPPED

¼ CUP FIRMLY PACKED FRESH CILANTRO LEAVES, COARSELY CHOPPED

1. Heat a wok or large nonstick sauté pan over medium heat for 40 seconds and then add the oil around the perimeter of the wok so that it coats the sides and bottom. When the surface shimmers slightly, after about 30 seconds, add the garlic, chiles, scallions, and salt and cook, stirring constantly, until the garlic is golden brown and fragrant, about 2 minutes.

2. Add the shrimp and stir-fry until it turns orange, about 2 minutes. Add the rice and cook, using a spatula to break up any clumps of rice and mixing the ingredients until well combined, about 4 minutes. Add the soy sauce, fish sauce, and sugar and cook for a few seconds.

3. Add the basil and cilantro leaves and cook until the leaves begin to wilt, about 30 seconds. Transfer the rice to a serving plate. Serve immediately.

Fragrant Herb Rice

This dish, referred to as *nasi kerabu* in Malay, is a specialty from the east coast of Malaysia. All the glorious fragrances from the Asian herb garden are combined subtly in this healthy dish. Enjoy as it is or as an accompaniment to Halibut Braised in Coconut Sambal (page 166).

SERVES 4 TO 6

3 CUPS JASMINE RICE

ONE 14-OUNCE CAN COCONUT MILK
(PAGE 26)

2 STALKS FRESH LEMONGRASS, SMASHED

ONE 3-INCH PIECE FRESH GALANGAL,
SMASHED

4 FRESH KAFFIR LIME LEAVES, STEMMED

1 TEASPOON SALT

⅓ CUP FRESH ASIAN SWEET BASIL
LEAVES, THINLY SLICED

⅓ CUP FRESH MINT LEAVES, THINLY
SLICED

⅓ CUP FRESH CILANTRO LEAVES, THINLY
SLICED

½ CUCUMBER, THINLY SLICED

1. Wash the rice by gently rubbing it with your fingers in a bowl filled with water. When the water becomes cloudy, drain the water and repeat the process until the water is clear. Drain and set the rice aside.

2. Combine the rice, 1½ cups water, and the coconut milk in a 4-quart saucepan over medium heat. Add the lemongrass, galangal, lime leaves, and salt and give it a good stir. Let the rice boil until steam holes appear in the rice and the surface looks dry, 6 to 7 minutes. Reduce the heat to low, cover the pot with a tight-fitting lid, and cook for 20 minutes.

3. Uncover and gently fluff the rice with a fork. Discard the lemongrass, galangal, and lime leaves. Fold in the basil, mint, cilantro, and cucumber. Serve immediately.

Indonesian Sambal Rice with Shrimp

Fried rice, or *nasi goreng,* is a common breakfast throughout Indonesia. It is often a simple way to use the leftover rice in your refrigerator; cooked rice is tossed with a seasoning sauce like sweet soy sauce and chile paste or sambal, as detailed in this recipe. It is usually topped with thinly sliced omelet and served with a cup of Javanese coffee. I have always found this dish to be a comforting quick snack.

SERVES 2

3 TABLESPOONS PLUS 1 TEASPOON CANOLA OR PEANUT OIL

1 LARGE EGG, BEATEN

⅓ CUP TRADITIONAL SAMBAL (PAGE 55)

1 LARGE SHALLOT, SLICED

2 GARLIC CLOVES, MINCED

½ TEASPOON SALT

1 TABLESPOON FRESH LIME JUICE

12 OUNCES LARGE SHRIMP, PEELED AND DEVEINED

3 CUPS PERFECT JASMINE RICE (PAGE 176)

2 TABLESPOONS SWEET SOY SAUCE

½ CUCUMBER, SLICED

1. Heat a wok or large nonstick sauté pan over medium heat for 40 seconds and then add 1 teaspoon of the oil around the perimeter of the wok so that it coats the sides and bottom. When the surface shimmers slightly, after about 30 seconds, pour in the beaten egg. Gently swirl the wok to coat it thinly with the egg; cook for 1 minute, until set. Remove the egg and slice into thin strips. Set aside.

2. Heat the remaining 3 tablespoons oil in the wok over medium heat until it shimmers, about 30 seconds. Add the sambal, shallot, garlic, salt, and lime juice. Cook, stirring frequently, until the oil separates and appears on the surface and the sambal has thickened and reduced in quantity, about 5 minutes.

3. Add the shrimp, raise the heat to high, and cook until the shrimp turn orange, about 2 minutes. Add the rice and sweet soy sauce and cook for 3 minutes, using a spatula to break up any clumps of rice and mixing the ingredients until well combined.

4. Remove from the heat and transfer to a serving platter. Garnish with the sliced omelet and sliced cucumber. Serve immediately.

Fresh Rice Noodles with Seafood and Basil

Known as *pad kee mao* in Thailand, this dish reminds me of spaghetti Bolognese in texture and appearance. The flavors, however, are purely Thai: a combination of sweet, sour, salty, and spicy. When I teach a noodle class, I always explain that there are three vital phases to getting the most flavor in your *pad kee mao*: the first is to season the oil with garlic, shallots, and chiles; the second is to flavor the noodles with fish sauce, sweet soy sauce, white pepper, and roasted chile paste to taste; and the third is to create overall bursts of freshness with basil leaves. That said, there is a lot of flexibility in preparing this seafood and noodle dish, and it seems that no two Thai cooks make it in quite the same way. SERVES 4

1 POUND FRESH RICE NOODLES (*KWAY TEOW*)

3 TABLESPOONS PEANUT OIL

4 GARLIC CLOVES, MINCED

2 LARGE SHALLOTS, SLICED

1 FRESH RED CHILE, SLICED

8 OUNCES LARGE SHRIMP, PEELED AND DEVEINED

8 OUNCES SQUID, CUT INTO RINGS

3 TABLESPOONS FISH SAUCE, OR TO TASTE

3 TABLESPOONS SWEET SOY SAUCE

⅛ TEASPOON FRESHLY GROUND WHITE PEPPER

1 TEASPOON ROASTED CHILE PASTE (PAGE 61)

1 CUP FIRMLY PACKED FRESH ASIAN SWEET BASIL LEAVES

1. Gently separate the rice noodles into individual strands, as they are quite sticky. Set aside.

2. Heat a wok or large nonstick sauté pan over medium heat for 40 seconds and then add the oil around the perimeter of the wok so that it coats the sides and bottom. When the surface shimmers slightly, after about 30 seconds, add the garlic, shallots, and chile and cook, stirring constantly, until the garlic appears golden brown and fragrant, 3 to 4 minutes. The chile should have transferred some of its natural red color to the oil by now. Add the shrimp and cook, stirring, for about 2 minutes. Add the squid and cook, stirring, for 1 minute.

3. Add the noodles, fish sauce, sweet soy sauce, white pepper, and roasted chile paste. Raise the heat to medium-high and cook, spreading the noodles evenly around the wok and placing the seafood over the noodles to avoid overcooking, until all the liquid has been absorbed by the noodles, 2 to 3 minutes. Taste and adjust the seasoning with fish sauce for desired saltiness.

4. Toss in the basil leaves and cook for 30 seconds until the basil is wilted. Serve immediately.

Pad Thai with Chicken

Pad thai, originally from Bangkok, has been perfected over the years in Thailand by cooks dishing out street food at roadside stands. There this great-tasting specialty has a balanced sweet, sour, salty, and spicy flavor. It is never oily or red from the use of ketchup, as is often the case at Western Thai restaurants. In this recipe, I use salted radish—made from pickled daikon—found at most Asian supermarkets. It adds an authentic salty and sweet taste to pad thai. If you cannot find the radish, omit it, as there really isn't a substitute. It is best to serve pad thai with an accompaniment made from fish sauce, hot red pepper flakes, cut lime, and some sugar in small individual bowls. SERVES 4

4 OUNCES DRIED RICE NOODLES (ALSO KNOWN AS *BANH PHO*)

3 TABLESPOONS FISH SAUCE, OR MORE TO TASTE

3 TABLESPOONS TAMARIND LIQUID (PAGE 35)

1 TABLESPOON SUGAR

1 TEASPOON DISTILLED WHITE VINEGAR

¼ CUP PLUS 1 ½ TEASPOONS CANOLA OR PEANUT OIL

4 OUNCES FIRM TOFU, DRAINED, PATTED DRY, AND DICED

4 GARLIC CLOVES, MINCED

1 LARGE SHALLOT, SLICED

1 TABLESPOON SALTED RADISH, CHOPPED

5 OUNCES BONELESS, SKINLESS CHICKEN BREAST, CUT INTO ½-INCH PIECES

1 TEASPOON PURE CHILE POWDER (PAGE 17) OR CAYENNE

1 LARGE EGG

½ CUP BEAN SPROUTS

3 SCALLIONS, BOTH WHITE AND GREEN PARTS, CHOPPED

3 TABLESPOONS CHOPPED UNSALTED ROASTED PEANUTS

1 LIME, QUARTERED

1. Soak the dried rice noodles in a large bowl filled with hot water for 30 to 40 minutes, or until the noodles turn white and limp. They will double in quantity, so make sure you have enough water to keep the noodles covered.

2. Meanwhile, prepare the sauce by combining the fish sauce, tamarind liquid, sugar, and vinegar in a medium bowl. Stir until the sugar dissolves; set aside.

3. Heat a wok or large nonstick sauté pan over medium-high heat for 40 seconds and then add ¼ cup of the oil around the perimeter of the wok so that it coats the sides and bottom. When the surface shimmers slightly, after about 30 seconds, add the tofu and cook for a few seconds before stirring. This way the tofu can brown properly and will be crisp. Cook the tofu in this manner until brown on all sides, 3 to 4 minutes.

4. Add the garlic, shallot, and salted radish and cook, stirring, until the garlic is golden brown, about 2 minutes.

5. Add the chicken and chile powder and cook, stirring, until the meat is no longer pink, 4 to 5 minutes. Drain the noodles, add them to the wok, and mix thoroughly. Pour in the sauce and cook, stirring, until all the seasoning sauce has been absorbed by the noodles, about 4 minutes. The noodles will begin to change texture and appear softer.

6. Push the noodles to one side of the wok and add the remaining 1½ teaspoons of oil to the center of the wok. Allow the oil to heat up for a few seconds, then break the egg into the oil. Avoid scrambling it. Instead, immediately bring the noodles on top of the egg and allow the egg to set on the bottom. Once the egg is cooked, after about 1 minute, stir and cook for 2 minutes.

7. Toss in the bean sprouts, scallions, and peanuts. Cook until the vegetables are wilted, about 1 minute. Taste and add fish sauce for saltiness if needed. Remove from the heat. Transfer to a serving platter and garnish with the quartered limes. Serve immediately.

Malaysia Market Noodles "*Satu char kway teow,* boss!"

Translated, this means "Boss, one plate of fried *kway teow,*" and it is the way millions of customers in Malaysia shout out their noodle orders to roadside peddlers. Prepared in minutes, this dish is stir-fried in a wok with a mix of ingredients that includes fresh rice noodles, an egg, and bean sprouts with sweet and salty soy sauce. This dish is great for a quick lunch or supper. I grew up with this noodle dish, and it is undoubtedly my favorite. SERVES 4

1 POUND FRESH RICE NOODLES (*KWAY TEOW*)

3 TABLESPOONS CANOLA OR PEANUT OIL

4 GARLIC CLOVES, MINCED

2 LARGE SHALLOTS, SLICED

1 FRESH RED CHILE, SLICED

8 OUNCES LARGE SHRIMP, PEELED AND DEVEINED

¼ CUP SOY SAUCE, OR MORE TO TASTE

2 TABLESPOONS SWEET SOY SAUCE

½ TEASPOON PURE CHILE POWDER (PAGE 17) OR CAYENNE

2 LARGE EGGS, BEATEN

1 CUP BEAN SPROUTS

½ CUP FRESH CHIVES, CHOPPED INTO ½-INCH PIECES

1. Gently separate the rice noodles into individual strands, as they are quite sticky. Set aside.

2. Heat a wok or large nonstick sauté pan over medium heat for 40 seconds and then add the oil around the perimeter of the wok so that it coats the sides and bottom. When the surface shimmers slightly, after about 30 seconds, add the garlic, shallots, and chile and cook, stirring, until fragrant, 3 to 4 minutes.

3. Add the shrimp and cook, stirring, for 2 minutes. Add the noodles, soy sauce, sweet soy sauce, and chile powder. Raise the heat to medium-high and cook, stirring, for 1 minute. Add the beaten eggs and cook, stirring, until the eggs are fully cooked, about 2 minutes. The noodles will no longer appear wet from the eggs when cooked.

4. Add the bean sprouts and chives and cook, stirring, for 3 minutes, until the vegetables are slightly wilted. Taste and adjust the flavors with soy sauce for the desired saltiness. Remove from the heat. Serve immediately.

Chutneys, Pickles, and Sambals

Green Mango Chutney

✦

Tomato Chutney

✦

Green Apple and Nutmeg Chutney

✦

Pineapple Pickle

✦

Penang-Style Vegetable Pickle

✦

Shallot and Lemongrass Sambal

✦

Lime and Chile Sambal

✦

Tomato Sambal

✦

Crispy Garlic Sambal

✦

Fried Shallots

Chutneys, pickles, and sambals, although not as grand as any main course, have held a special place in my heart since childhood. Growing up under my mother's culinary tutelage, I have come to appreciate the powerful significance of these tasty condiments.

I learned early that chutneys enhance digestion and add an interesting twist to the taste of food. Normally made from the pulp of seasonal fruits and selected spices, each spoonful magically gives the food you're consuming a multidimensional flavor. Chutneys were a hit at my mother's spice stall in the Central Market. On school breaks, I observed how eagerly her customers carted away jars and sometimes whole crates of my mother's famous mango chutney. Though it was time consuming to make, my mother took the extra effort to make the chutney to keep her customers happy. Many became good friends, including Aunt Dolly, a petite woman in thick spectacles and dressed to the hilt in brightly colored clothes, who always came to buy my mother's mango chutney and would buy her spices at the same time.

My mother had learned the mango chutney recipe from my grandmother, Annya, who taught her the secrets of combining just the right spices with unripe mangoes in season. My grandmother's chutneys had a faithful following throughout the little town of Ipoh, about four hours from Kuala Lumpur. Ipoh began as a small harbor town along the Kinta River, a trading stop for junks and sampans navigating the Straits of Malacca, and it retains an air of grandeur from its past.

Every year, my family would take a trip to Ipoh to visit Annya's old mango villa out in the country. There was a certain mystique about my grandmother's home, surrounded by thick vegetation and overlooking the distant hills. Annya had a very large lot where a few chickens ran freely and many tropical fruit trees grew, including mango, papaya, rambutan, guava, and banana.

The villa had a long veranda with timber floors that ran the length of the kitchen. Knowing that the villa would soon be filled with children, Annya would have already placed lots of lime in large trays for my brother, my cousins, and I to squeeze into a huge pot until our fingers hurt. But we were not bothered by the effort as we would soon be rewarded with her luscious mango pudding.

Once the juice is squeezed out of the lime, the halved fruit is said to be less tart and to dry out faster in the sun. For a month, the sun-dried limes are soaked in vinegar and salt and added to ground dried chiles, mustard seeds, and other spices cooked in oil. These lime pickles were later sold in our spice stall too. In the spice trade, making pickles on the side was a natural advantage for my mother.

Just as much as we enjoyed making chutneys and pickles, we also loved our sambals. They are served as a condiment on the side the way salt and pepper are at a Western meal. A handful of red chiles, garlic, sweet tomatoes, and pungent shrimp paste are all the basic ingredients needed for a good homemade sambal. Its pungency takes a little getting used to, but once you have developed the taste there is no ridding yourself of the addiction. Most Malaysians and Indonesians dish out sambal in a little bowl to be eaten according to one's preference, with steaming hot rice and curries or vegetables. Sambal also stimulates the appetite and fills the mouth with lots of flavor.

In this chapter, I share my family's recipes for perfect chutneys, pickles, and sambals and hope you'll enjoy them as a crescendo to a good meal.

Green Mango Chutney

This is my grandmother's recipe. Where she used tiny green unripe mangoes, which are difficult to find in America, I use the large partly ripe green mangoes sold at most supermarkets. The mangoes are cooked in vinegar and brown sugar until they turn thick and jamlike. A burst of flavors comes alive at the end when ground, toasted spices are added to the cooked mangoes. My annya never used oil in making this chutney; according to her, it preserves longer without it. MAKES 2 CUPS

---

4 GREEN (UNRIPE) MANGOES (ABOUT 3 POUNDS), PEELED AND CUT INTO 2-INCH PIECES

2 CUPS CIDER VINEGAR

ONE 2-INCH CINNAMON STICK

¼ TEASPOON CLOVES

2¼ CUPS BROWN SUGAR

⅛ TEASPOON MUSTARD SEEDS

⅛ TEASPOON CUMIN SEEDS

1 DRIED RED CHILE, BROKEN INTO SMALL PIECES OR CRUSHED

---

1. Combine the mangoes, vinegar, cinnamon, cloves, and brown sugar in a heavy 4-quart saucepan and bring to a boil over medium heat. Cook for 10 minutes. Stir and then reduce the heat to low. Allow the mangoes to cook until soft and most of the liquid evaporates, about 1½ hours. The mixture will become thick and jamlike when done.

2. Meanwhile, put the mustard seeds, cumin seeds, and chile in a small skillet over medium heat. Immediately cover with a splatter screen to prevent the mustard seeds from popping out of the pan. When the mustard seeds stop popping, after 30 to 40 seconds, remove the screen and cook the spices until the chile darkens, 1 to 2 minutes. Remove from the heat.

3. Pound the spices to a powder in a mortar with a pestle or grind them in a coffee or spice grinder. Add the ground spices to the mango mixture and stir well. Cook for 1 minute. Remove from the heat. Store the chutney in an airtight glass jar in the refrigerator for up to 2 weeks. Serve at room temperature.

Cook's Tip *For longer storage or gift giving, chutneys can be ladled into sterilized pint canning jars, leaving ¼ inch headspace. Screw on the lid and process in boiling water in a canner for at least 10 minutes.*

Tomato Chutney Like salsa, this chutney made from fresh tomatoes can be served as a side dish or as a dip. The cinnamon and cumin seeds give the chutney a sweet aroma. I usually enjoy the chutney the day it is made, with Saffron Pilaf. At home before our Sunday gatherings, my family would eat this chutney with leftover curries. MAKES 1½ CUPS

3 TABLESPOONS EXTRA VIRGIN OLIVE OIL

¼ TEASPOON MUSTARD SEEDS

¼ TEASPOON CUMIN SEEDS

ONE 2-INCH CINNAMON STICK

5 TOMATOES, QUARTERED

¼ TEASPOON GROUND TURMERIC

¼ TEASPOON PURE CHILE POWDER (PAGE 17) OR CAYENNE

¼ CUP BROWN SUGAR

1 TABLESPOON RAISINS

¼ TEASPOON SALT

1. Heat the oil in a medium saucepan over medium heat. Add the mustard seeds and immediately cover with a splatter screen to prevent the mustard seeds from popping out of the pan. When the mustard seeds stop popping, after 30 to 40 seconds, add the cumin seeds and cinnamon. Cook for 30 seconds and then add the tomatoes, turmeric, chile powder, and brown sugar. Cook, stirring every so often, for 20 minutes, until the tomatoes have broken down.

2. Add the raisins and salt. For moist chutney, cook for another 5 minutes. For thick, jamlike chutney, cook for 10 minutes longer, or until the chutney appears glazed. Store the chutney in an airtight glass jar in the refrigerator for up to 3 days or in the freezer for 1 month. Serve warm.

Green Apple and Nutmeg Chutney

This chutney is quite similar to Green Mango Chutney (page 194). I normally prepare it during the autumn months, when apples are plentiful and fresh in Washington. Be prepared to have your kitchen smelling like hot apple pie. I love to serve this chutney with most curries. You may also add some of this chutney to your favorite sandwich for a lovely bite. MAKES 2 CUPS

4 GREEN APPLES, PEELED, CORED, AND CUT INTO 2-INCH PIECES

1 CUP DISTILLED VINEGAR

ONE 2-INCH CINNAMON STICK

¼ TEASPOON CLOVES

1 TEASPOON FRESHLY GRATED NUTMEG

1½ CUPS BROWN SUGAR

⅛ TEASPOON MUSTARD SEEDS

⅛ TEASPOON CUMIN SEEDS

1 DRIED RED CHILE, BROKEN INTO SMALL PIECES

1. Combine the apples, vinegar, cinnamon, cloves, nutmeg, and brown sugar in a heavy 4-quart saucepan over medium heat and bring to a boil. Boil for 15 minutes, reduce the heat to low, and stir. Allow the apples to cook until soft and most of the liquid evaporates, about 45 minutes. The mixture will become thick and jamlike.

2. Put the mustard seeds, cumin seeds, and chile in a small skillet over medium heat. Immediately cover with a splatter screen to prevent the mustard seeds from popping out of the pan. When the mustard seeds stop popping, after 30 to 40 seconds, remove the screen and cook until the chile darkens, 1 to 2 minutes. Remove from the heat.

3. Pound the spices to a powder in a mortar with a pestle or grind them in a coffee or spice grinder. Add the ground spices to the apple mixture and stir well. Cook for 1 minute. Remove from the heat. Store the chutney in an airtight glass jar in the refrigerator for up to 2 weeks. For longer storage or gift giving, see Cook's Tip, page 194. Serve at room temperature.

Pineapple Pickle This tangy condiment, also known as *achar,* meaning pickle in Malaysian, is often eaten as a relish. In many vegetarian restaurants, pineapple pickle is served on the side with hot rice, vegetables, and a smorgasbord of curry. I serve this dish during barbecue parties in the summer—pineapples perfectly complement the hot weather. This salsalike pickle is best served with Lemon Pepper Wings (page 72), Chicken Satay (page 82), or any grilled dish. You can also substitute ripe mangoes for the pineapples and serve this as a dip with rice crackers. MAKES 3 CUPS

½ PINEAPPLE, PEELED, CORED, AND CUT INTO ½-INCH CUBES

1 MEDIUM ENGLISH CUCUMBER, PEELED, SEEDED, AND DICED

2 SMALL SHALLOTS, THINLY SLICED

¼ CUP DISTILLED WHITE VINEGAR

2 TABLESPOONS SUGAR

2 TABLESPOONS FRESH LIME JUICE

1 FRESH RED CHILE, HALVED AND SLICED

½ TEASPOON SALT

Combine the pineapple, cucumber, shallots, vinegar, sugar, lime juice, chile, and salt in a bowl and mix thoroughly. The pickle can be made up to 1 hour in advance and refrigerated. Serve at room temperature.

Penang-Style Vegetable Pickle This piquant northern Malaysian delicacy called *nonya achar* was introduced to me by my aunty, a neighbor, who made it at home on a regular basis. We could always tell when she was making *achar* from the scent of vinegar swirling in the air. She would call me over and hand me a bowl filled with pieces of cucumber, carrot, and cabbage bathing in a sweet and tangy peanut mixture, still warm as I carried it home to enjoy with my family. This pickle goes well with all rice-based dishes. MAKES 3 CUPS

½ CUCUMBER

¾ TO 1 TEASPOON SALT

1 ½ CUPS DISTILLED WHITE VINEGAR

8 OUNCES CARROTS, CUT INTO 2-INCH-LONG PIECES

1 CUP ROUGHLY CHOPPED GREEN CABBAGE

3 TO 4 FRESH RED CHILES, SEEDED AND CHOPPED

6 GARLIC CLOVES

3 TABLESPOONS SUGAR, OR MORE TO TASTE

¾ CUP UNSALTED ROASTED PEANUTS

3 TABLESPOONS VEGETABLE OIL

1 ½ TABLESPOONS SESAME SEEDS

1. Quarter the cucumber lengthwise and then cut into 2-inch-long strips (leave the skin on). Put in a bowl and add ¼ teaspoon of the salt to help draw the water out of the cucumber. Set aside.

2. To blanch the vegetables, bring the vinegar and 1 cup water to a boil in a 4-quart saucepan over high heat. Squeeze as much water as possible from the cucumber pieces. Add the cucumber pieces to the pot and cook for 2 minutes. Remove the cucumber pieces with a slotted spoon and place in a colander to drain further.

3. Bring the vinegar mixture to a boil again and, working in small batches, add the carrots and cook for 3 minutes. Remove with a slotted spoon and place the carrots into the colander.

4. Next, add the cabbage and cook for 2 minutes. Remove and transfer to a colander.

5. Combine the chiles, garlic, sugar, and the remaining ½ to ¾ teaspoon salt in a food processor and process to a paste. Remove and set aside in a bowl. Put the peanuts into the same food processor (it is not necessary to rinse the processor) and process until the peanuts are finely ground. Set aside in a separate bowl.

6. Heat the oil in a small saucepan. Add the spice paste and cook for 10 minutes, until oil appears on the surface. Add the ground peanuts and ⅓ cup water. Cook until the mixture thickens and appears glazed, about 5 minutes. The mixture should taste tangy yet a little sweet. Add a little more sugar if the mixture is too spicy. Remove from the heat.

7. Transfer the vegetables to a large bowl. Add the hot peanut mixture and sesame seeds. Toss the vegetables with a spoon until completely coated with the peanut mixture. Let cool. The pickle can be stored in an airtight glass jar in the refrigerator for up to 2 weeks. Serve at room temperature.

Cook's Tip *The longer the vegetable pickle sits, the tastier it gets.*

Shallot and Lemongrass Sambal Known in Bali as

sambal matah, this sambal exudes the heavenly scent of lemongrass, with each bite delivering a citruslike flavor. To enjoy the delicate texture of the lemongrass, peel several fibrous outer layers until the soft inner part is revealed. A teaspoon or two of this sambal goes well with grilled seafood dishes, especially Fragrant Seafood Cakes (page 84), and also makes a wonderful accompaniment to summer salads.
MAKES ½ CUP

1 LARGE SHALLOT, THINLY SLICED	½ TEASPOON SALT
3 STALKS FRESH LEMONGRASS, INNER PART THINLY SLICED	⅛ TEASPOON FRESHLY GROUND BLACK PEPPER
2 FRESH RED CHILES, THINLY SLICED	1½ TABLESPOONS PEANUT OIL
JUICE OF 1 LIME	
½ TEASPOON SHRIMP PASTE, TOASTED (PAGE 34)	

Combine the shallot, lemongrass, chiles, lime juice, shrimp paste, salt, pepper, and oil in a bowl and mix until the shrimp paste is completely dissolved. The sambal will keep for up to 2 days in the refrigerator. Serve at room temperature.

Lime and Chile Sambal

This lime and chile sambal, known as *sambal belachan*, has a distinctly Malaysian aroma and taste. This exotic dip is usually made fresh daily and spiked with freshly squeezed kalamansi lime juice just before being served. I have changed the recipe to accommodate regular limes; however, if you do find frozen kalamansi lime juice in Asian stores, use it. This sambal is consumed in small quantities—a teaspoon to a tablespoon at a time—but once you have savored it, you'll come back for more. MAKES ¼ CUP

3 FRESH RED CHILES, SEEDED AND MINCED

1 TEASPOON SHRIMP PASTE, TOASTED (PAGE 34)

½ TEASPOON SALT

¼ TEASPOON SUGAR

1 TABLESPOON FRESH LIME JUICE

Pound the chiles, shrimp paste, salt, and sugar to a paste in a mortar with a pestle. Add the lime juice and mix well. Transfer to a small serving bowl. The sambal will keep for up to 2 days in the refrigerator. Serve at room temperature.

Tomato Sambal I love the taste of this dish, known as *sambal tomat* in Bali. At home, I serve it with grilled seafood or tofu and steamed veggies. It has a wonderful smoky sweet flavor and a subtle taste of pepper. MAKES 1 ½ CUPS

¼ CUP VEGETABLE OIL

8 GARLIC CLOVES, CHOPPED

4 SMALL SHALLOTS, SLICED

2 TO 3 FRESH RED CHILES, SEEDED AND CHOPPED

3 TOMATOES, SEEDED AND CHOPPED

1 TEASPOON SHRIMP PASTE, TOASTED (PAGE 34)

½ TEASPOON SALT, OR TO TASTE

1 TEASPOON FRESHLY GROUND BLACK PEPPER

2 TABLESPOONS SUGAR, OR TO TASTE

1. Heat the oil in a small skillet over medium heat. Add the garlic and cook until golden brown, 3 minutes. Remove and set aside. In the same oil, cook the shallots until light brown, about 5 minutes. Remove and set aside.

2. Add the chiles, tomatoes, and shrimp paste to the pan and cook until the tomatoes are soft and aromatic, 2 to 3 minutes. Remove and set aside to cool.

3. Combine the garlic, shallots, and tomato mixture in a food processor and blend to a coarse paste. Transfer to a bowl and season with salt, pepper, and sugar, stirring to dissolve the sugar. Taste, adding more sugar if the sambal tastes too spicy. The sambal can be stored in an airtight glass jar in the refrigerator for up to 4 days. Serve at room temperature.

Crispy Garlic Sambal

This garlicky sambal is one of my favorites and is always present when I am eating fried rice or noodles, ready to add an extra oomph. MAKES ¼ CUP

¼ CUP PEANUT OIL

8 GARLIC CLOVES, MINCED

5 TABLESPOONS SWEET SOY SAUCE

1 TABLESPOON FRESH LIME JUICE

---

1. Heat a wok or small nonstick sauté pan over medium heat for 40 seconds and then add the oil around the perimeter of the wok so that it coats the sides and bottom. When the surface shimmers slightly, after about 30 seconds, add the garlic and cook, stirring constantly, until golden brown and crisp, about 3 minutes. Remove the garlic with a slotted spoon to a bowl. Discard the oil.

2. Add the sweet soy sauce and lime juice to the hot garlic and mix well to incorporate the ingredients. The sambal can be made up to 1 day in advance and stored in an airtight glass jar at room temperature. Serve at room temperature.

Fried Shallots Early morning in Malaysia, traders unload huge bamboo baskets full of tiny shallots and other fresh spices along the narrow streets of Kuala Lumpur's Chow Kit market. The streets bustle with small shops selling local delicacies from coconut cakes to steaming bowls of noodles with shallots. Fried shallots are an important table condiment in Southeast Asian cuisine and present at most meals. They are valued for their delicate sweet flavor and warming fragrance. Even a teaspoon of fried shallots will improve the taste of fried noodles, rice dishes, soups, and salads. The shallot-infused oil also imparts delicious flavors, especially when added to soups and salad dressings. I keep a bowl of fried shallots on my kitchen table to eat every day with every meal. MAKES 1 CUP

8 OUNCES SHALLOTS, THINLY SLICED	½ CUP CANOLA OR PEANUT OIL
½ TEASPOON SALT	

1. Heat a wok or small nonstick sauté pan over medium heat for 40 seconds and then add the oil around the perimeter of the wok so that it coats the sides and bottom. When the surface shimmers slightly, after about 30 seconds, add the shallots and salt and cook until golden brown and crisp, 7 minutes.

2. Remove the shallots with a slotted spoon and let cool on a paper towel. Place the shallots in an airtight container and store at room temperature for up to 1 day.

Cook's Tip To make peeling easier, soak the shallots in salt and water for 5 minutes to soften the skin. Drain the shallots and dry them on a paper tower before slicing.

Desserts

Cinnamon Chocolate Cake

✦

Rich Chocolate Cardamom Cakes

✦

Sunday Crêpes with Coconut Syrup

✦

Coconut Agar-Agar

✦

Black Rice Pudding

✦

Coconut Flan Infused with Star Anise

✦

Jasmine Cake

✦

Semolina Tea Cake with Raisins

✦

Monsoon Rice Pudding

✦

Pumpkin Coconut Pudding

When I think of desserts, I reminisce about monsoon downpours and thunderstorm retreats. It was amazing when the sky snarled, running its blue into a thousand shades of grays to black. After a magical display of eye-piercing streaks, its deep rumble deafened, and sheets of water drenched the roads and turned them into milky, tea-colored streams.

When it rained for days on end during the monsoon season, I felt as if the whole sky was falling down and I would burrow into the safety of my home, resigned to watch the thunderstorm pelt its rage. But besides the sights and sounds of the downpour, there was something else—a peculiar way the kitchen would beckon me for desserts.

In the sanctuary of the kitchen, my mother and I would be drawn to our old mirrored cupboard like bees to honey, rummaging through canned coconut milk, flour, vanilla, eggs, agar-agar, palm sugar, cocoa, and other tins to make desserts. With the fresh markets closed for business, we had to depend on our provisions in the pantry to comfort our cravings. My favorite was coconut agar-agar, a classic Southeast Asian dessert made from coconut milk, sugar, vegetable gelatin or agar-agar, and fragrant pandan leaves. I loved stirring the coconut mixture and drawing in the fragrance of the pandan leaves. When the coconut agar-agar was cooked, I would chill it in the refrigerator until set. Then I would delicately cut it into diamond shapes and neatly arrange them on a silver tray. My favorite part was nibbling on the edges that didn't quite make a perfect diamond shape.

Meanwhile, my mother would stir grains of basmati rice as they simmered in milk and vanilla bean in a small pot on the stove, checking the consistency and making sure they were cooked perfectly. After a few minutes our kitchen was filled with the sweet scent of vanilla. We poured our warm rice pudding into little bowls and enjoyed this nutritious dish, sharing some close moments only a mother and daughter can cherish forever. Now that I reside in the Pacific Northwest, when it rains, my heart still desires for the tropical tastes of my childhood.

The recipes in this chapter are for the everyday desserts I love. They can be made quickly and easily with ingredients available at most grocery stores. For me, each one of these desserts can be an indulgent complement to a meal. When I cook spicy Thai food for friends, for instance, I treat them to Coconut Agar-Agar as a refreshing palate cleanser. For a Saturday barbecue, I am passionate about Coconut Flan Infused with Star Anise, and when I want to impress, I know it has to be Cinnamon Chocolate Cake. As I see it, desserts are sweet endings to a meal and a great start to pleasant conversations.

Pandan plants

Cinnamon Chocolate Cake

Sensuous and delicious, this recipe was created by my lifelong friend Sumithra, an ex-lawyer who opened a gourmet bakery in Kuala Lumpur. As teenagers, we would spend many afternoons baking in my home, sharing stories that brought our friendship even closer. I have altered this cake just a little to enhance its flavor with a hint of spice. This is our favorite chocolate cake, and I hope it will become your favorite too. SERVES 8

Cake

4 OUNCES FINE-QUALITY BITTERSWEET CHOCOLATE, BROKEN INTO SMALL PIECES

1¾ CUPS PLUS 1 TABLESPOON (3 STICKS PLUS 5 TABLESPOONS) UNSALTED BUTTER, AT ROOM TEMPERATURE

1 CUP ALL-PURPOSE FLOUR

½ CUP PLUS 1½ TABLESPOONS UNSWEETENED COCOA POWDER

1½ CUPS SUGAR

5 LARGE EGGS

3 LARGE EGG YOLKS

1 TEASPOON SWEETENED CONDENSED MILK MIXED WITH ½ CUP PLUS 1 TABLESPOON COLD WATER

2 TEASPOONS VANILLA EXTRACT

Glaze

12 OUNCES FINE-QUALITY BITTERSWEET CHOCOLATE, BROKEN INTO SMALL PIECES

½ CUP HEAVY CREAM

½ TEASPOON GROUND CINNAMON

1. Preheat the oven to 325°F. Lightly butter a 9-inch round cake pan. Sprinkle the inside of the pan with flour and rotate the pan to coat the sides and bottom evenly. Tap out any excess flour. Set aside.

2. To make the cake, melt the chocolate and 5 tablespoons of the butter in a double boiler over medium-low heat. Set aside to cool.

3. Sift together the flour and cocoa and set aside.

4. Beat the remaining 1½ cups (3 sticks) butter and the sugar with an electric mixer on medium speed until creamy and light in color. Add the whole eggs one at a time, beating until incorporated after each addition. Next add the egg yolks and beat for 1 minute. Scrape down the sides of the bowl with a rubber spatula. Mix again for 20 seconds.

5. Reduce the speed to low. Add the flour mixture a little at a time, alternating with the sweetened condensed milk mixture, beating until incorporated after each addition. Add the melted chocolate and butter and beat until incorporated, about 30 seconds. Add the vanilla and mix until incorporated.

6. Spoon the batter into the prepared pan, smoothing out the top with the back of a spoon. Bake for 1 hour and 10 minutes, or until the cake begins to come away from the sides of the pan, the cake springs back when touched, and a toothpick inserted in the center of the cake comes out clean.

7. Remove the pan from the oven. Cool the cake completely on a rack. Run a knife around the edges of the pan. Place a flat plate on the pan. Holding the plate and pan firmly, invert with one quick motion. Remove the pan and allow the cake to cool completely.

8. To make the glaze, melt the chocolate, cream, and cinnamon in a double boiler over low heat. Stir until the chocolate is completely melted. Set aside to cool completely, 10 to 15 minutes.

9. Using a metal spatula, spread the glaze evenly across the cake, allowing it to drip down the sides. Serve at room temperature. Leftovers can be wrapped in plastic wrap and kept at room temperature for up to 2 days.

Rich Chocolate Cardamom Cakes

I am a chocoholic, and when it comes to chocolate cake, it has to be irresistibly rich to satisfy my cravings. To make these cakes, buy fine-quality chocolate with cocoa beans, not sugar, as the first ingredient. I have added cardamom to this recipe, which accentuates the chocolate taste and gives the cakes a mochalike aroma without adding coffee. SERVES 5

8 OUNCES FINE-QUALITY BITTERSWEET CHOCOLATE, BROKEN INTO SMALL PIECES

1 CUP (2 STICKS) UNSALTED BUTTER, AT ROOM TEMPERATURE

½ CUP CONFECTIONERS' SUGAR, PLUS MORE FOR DUSTING

4 LARGE EGGS, SEPARATED, AT ROOM TEMPERATURE

½ TEASPOON GROUND CARDAMOM

½ CUP ALL-PURPOSE FLOUR, SIFTED

1. Preheat the oven to 350°F. Lightly butter five 6-ounce ovenproof ramekins and dust lightly with flour. Set aside.

2. Melt the chocolate in a double boiler over medium-low heat. Set aside to cool.

3. Meanwhile, beat the butter and sugar with an electric mixer on medium speed until creamy and airy. Scrape down the sides of the bowl with a rubber spatula if needed. Add the eggs yolks one at a time and continue to beat the mixture until it has doubled in volume. Add the cardamom and beat for 1 minute.

4. Stir in the melted chocolate and beat for 1 minute. Fold in the flour and mix until well combined.

5. Whip the eggs whites to stiff peaks with an electric mixer. Fold the whites into the cake mixture until you have a smooth batter. Spoon the mixture into the prepared ramekins and then place the ramekins on a baking sheet. Bake for 30 minutes, until firm to the touch on the outside but slightly moist inside; a toothpick inserted in the center should come out with moist crumbs attached.

6. Cool the cakes completely on a rack. Run a knife around the edges of the ramekins, then invert. Dust with confectioners' sugar if desired.

Sunday Crêpes with Coconut Syrup

My children and their friends love these deliciously delicate crêpes eaten hot off the pan and made in quick succession to keep up with the children's ravenous appetites. You don't need a crêpe pan to make these, as they turn out great in a regular nonstick skillet. I use the bottom side of a ladle to gently spread the batter thinly in a circular motion, but you may tilt the pan to swirl the batter if you prefer. Finally, a little butter is thinly spread on each crêpe just before turning it over. Different in look and taste from French crêpes, these crêpes end up with an appealing golden circular pattern on them. MAKES 8 CRÊPES

2 CUPS WHOLE MILK

3 LARGE EGGS

2 TABLESPOONS SUGAR

1 CUP PLUS 3 TABLESPOONS ALL-PURPOSE FLOUR

⅛ TEASPOON GROUND CINNAMON

4 TABLESPOONS (½ STICK) UNSALTED BUTTER

¼ CUP PURE MAPLE SYRUP

¼ CUP CANNED COCONUT MILK (PAGE 26)

1. Put the milk, eggs, and sugar in a large bowl and whisk until combined. Add the flour and cinnamon and whisk again until the flour is totally incorporated. You will end up with a thin batter. Set aside.

2. Heat a medium nonstick skillet over medium heat. Add just a little butter and heat it until it sizzles. Ladle about ½ cup (use a measuring cup if you like) of batter into the pan, then tilt the pan and swirl the batter to form a thin, even round crêpe. Cook for a few seconds.

3. Add about ¼ teaspoon of butter to the crêpe and spread it around gently. Cook until the underside becomes golden brown, 2 to 3 minutes. Flip the crêpes using a flat spatula and cook the other side for 30 seconds, or until golden brown. Remove and set on a serving plate. Repeat until the batter is used up.

4. To make the coconut syrup, mix together the maple syrup and coconut milk and warm in the microwave or on the stovetop. Serve on the side with the crêpes, for spooning on top.

Coconut Agar-Agar This is the perfect finale for any spicy meal. The cooling sensation of coconut agar-agar instantly cleanses your palate with a burst of freshness. To ensure your agar-agar (which means "jelly" in Malaysia) sets perfectly, always dissolve it in hot water and never directly in boiling water. You'll find agar-agar, which is derived from seaweed and packed with calcium, at most Asian or gourmet markets. These clear crinkly strands are sealed in plastic packets and also sold in powder form. This dessert is an all-time favorite with my cooking classes. SERVES 6

1 FRESH OR FROZEN PANDAN LEAF (OPTIONAL), CUT IN HALF

¼ CUP AGAR-AGAR

½ CUP SUGAR

1 ½ CUPS CANNED COCONUT MILK (PAGE 26)

3 TABLESPOONS EVAPORATED MILK

1 CUP PEELED, CORED, AND CHOPPED FRESH PINEAPPLE

1. Bring 3 cups water and the pandan leaf if using to a boil in a medium saucepan over medium heat.

2. Separately, dissolve the agar-agar in ¼ cup hot water. Stir the mixture into the boiling water and cook, stirring, for 2 minutes.

3. Add the sugar and coconut milk and stir until the sugar dissolves. Bring just to a boil and immediately remove from the heat. Discard the pandan leaf.

4. Add the evaporated milk and stir well. Pour the mixture into a 9 x 12-inch glass baking dish. Set aside to cool thoroughly before chilling in the refrigerator for at least 2 hours or overnight.

5. Cut into squares and serve cold with fresh pineapple.

Black Rice Pudding

Most people who taste black sticky rice for the first time find it exceptionally delicious. Gluten free and high in fiber and antioxidants, this unmilled rice actually appears a deep burgundy color when cooked. You'll need to plan a day ahead to make this traditional recipe because glutinous rice needs to be soaked before cooking. SERVES 6

1 CUP BLACK GLUTINOUS RICE

⅓ CUP PLUS 3 TABLESPOONS SUGAR

1 ½ CUPS CANNED COCONUT MILK (PAGE 26)

1 TEASPOON SALT

2 TABLESPOONS RICE FLOUR OR CORNSTARCH MIXED WITH 2 TABLESPOONS WATER

1. Wash the rice by gently rubbing the grains with your fingers in a bowl of water. When the water becomes cloudy, drain the water and repeat the process until the water is clear. Drain the rice and add 2 cups of water. Allow the rice to soak overnight.

2. When ready to cook, drain the rice and place it in a saucepan with 1 quart water. Bring to a boil over high heat. Reduce the heat to medium-low and simmer the rice for 30 to 40 minutes, stirring intermittently to prevent the rice from burning and sticking. Add 2 more cups water and ⅓ cup of the sugar and cook for 10 minutes. As the rice cooks, it will crack open, become thicker, and appear burgundy in color.

3. Meanwhile, combine the coconut milk, the remaining 3 tablespoons sugar, the salt, and the rice flour in a medium saucepan over medium-low heat. Stir constantly to dissolve the sugar and to thicken the sauce. When the sauce begins to coat the ladle, after about 5 minutes, remove it from the heat.

4. Pour ½ cup of the coconut sauce into the black sticky rice and mix well. Pour the remainder into a bowl and reserve for serving.

5. To serve, spoon the sticky rice into individual bowls and top with the coconut sauce. Serve warm.

Coconut Flan Infused with Star Anise

When I was growing up, my mother used to keep a small wooden bowl filled with a potpourri of star anise and freshly picked jasmine flowers near the entrance of our home. "When visitors leave," she would say, "they'll pick up a star anise or a flower, and because of its sweet scent, they will say sweet things about the family."

Star anise is a dried star-shaped fruit from a tall evergreen tree indigenous to northern Vietnam. This reddish brown spice is used in many Southeast Asian desserts and drinks for its aromatic scent and savory taste. In this recipe, when the star anise is simmered in milk, the essential oils from the star anise are released to impart a hint of licorice anise flavor; the result is simply marvelous. I like to serve this dessert after a full-flavored meal such as Peppered Beef Salad (page 90) or Garlic Prawns (page 162), as the silky smooth texture seems light and refreshes the palate. SERVES 4

¾ CUP SUGAR

ONE 2-INCH CINNAMON STICK, BROKEN IN HALF

1 ½ CUPS WHOLE MILK

1 ½ CUPS CANNED COCONUT MILK (PAGE 26)

5 STAR ANISE

5 LARGE EGGS, BEATEN

1. Combine ½ cup water with ½ cup of the sugar and the cinnamon in a medium heavy saucepan over low heat. Stir to dissolve the sugar before the mixture reaches a boil. Use a wet pastry brush to push down any sugars that stick to the side of the pan. Boil without stirring until the mixture turns a light brown color, about 5 minutes. Remove from the heat. Use a slotted spoon to carefully discard the cinnamon.

2. Immediately pour about 2 tablespoons of the caramel into each of four 6-ounce ramekins. Tilt each ramekin to coat the bottom evenly. Place the ramekins in a baking pan and set aside. Preheat the oven to 350°F.

3. Combine the milk, coconut milk, and star anise in a medium saucepan over medium heat and bring just to a boil. Reduce the heat to low, add the remaining ¼ cup sugar, and stir to dissolve. Simmer the milk gently for 10 minutes, stirring occasionally. The mixture will appear slightly pale yellow in color when the spices are completely infused. Remove from the heat.

4. Whisk the eggs in a large bowl and slowly pour the hot milk into the eggs, whisking constantly.

5. Pour the custard through a fine-mesh strainer into a large measuring cup. Pour into the caramel-coated ramekins. Pour hot water into the baking pan to reach halfway up the sides of the ramekins.

6. Bake for about 40 minutes, or until the custards are almost set but still slightly jellylike in the center. Remove the baking pan from the oven and let the custards cool in the pan.

7. Serve warm or cold. For cold custard, refrigerate for at least 2 hours or overnight. Before serving, run a small knife around the edge of each custard and invert onto plates.

Jasmine Cake

Jasmine Cake I grow jasmine in my backyard in Seattle, and from summer to early autumn these beautiful clusters of fragrant white flowers remind me of my morning walks back in Kuala Lumpur. During my walks, I loved to watch residents picking these flowers and placing them in little bowls. The scent of jasmine immediately relaxes me, which is why I absolutely love baking this cake. When I offer a slice of this cake to a friend, the fragrance alone brings a smile. Serve this delicious cake with a medley of tropical fruits and a cup of chamomile tea. SERVES 12

2 CUPS ALL-PURPOSE FLOUR, SIFTED

1 TEASPOON BAKING SODA

2½ CUPS (5 STICKS) UNSALTED BUTTER, AT ROOM TEMPERATURE

1½ CUPS SUGAR

2 TABLESPOONS GRATED FRESH ORANGE ZEST

4 LARGE EGGS

¾ CUP FRESH ORANGE JUICE

1 TEASPOON JASMINE EXTRACT

1. Preheat the oven to 325°F. Lightly butter a 9-inch round cake pan. Sprinkle the inside of the pan with flour and rotate the pan to coat the sides and bottom evenly. Tap out any excess flour. Set aside.

2. Sift together the flour and baking soda. Set aside.

3. Beat the butter, sugar, and orange zest with an electric mixer on medium speed until creamy and light in color. Scrape down the sides of the bowl with a rubber spatula and beat again until smooth. Add the eggs one at a time, beating after each addition until well combined.

4. Reduce the speed to low. Add the flour mixture, alternating with the orange juice, mixing until incorporated after each addition. Add the jasmine extract and mix until incorporated.

5. Spoon the batter into the prepared pan, smoothing out the top with the back of the spoon. Bake for 1 hour and 20 minutes, or until the cake begins to come away from the sides of the pan, the cake springs back when touched, and a toothpick inserted in the center of the cake comes out clean.

6. Remove the pan from the oven. Cool the cake completely on a rack. Run a sharp knife around the edges of the pan. Place a flat plate on the pan. Holding the plate and pan firmly, invert with one quick motion. Remove the pan and allow the cake to cool completely. Serve at room temperature.

Cook's Tip *The jasmine extract does not impart any flavor to the cake, just a heavenly scent. The liquid is clear, labeled* Arome de Jasmin *or* Mali essence, *and is made of pure extract of the jasmine flower. Look for it at most Southeast Asian grocery stores.*

Semolina Tea Cake with Raisins

As a child, I enjoyed this cake, called *kaseri*, a common dessert served in Malaysian Indian homes during tea or after dinner. Traditionally, Malaysian mothers used a lot of butter to make this dish. I have since altered the recipe with the addition of milk and saffron to balance the taste. The resulting cake is much healthier yet equally delicious.

SERVES 12

5 TABLESPOONS UNSALTED BUTTER	**1 CUP WHOLE MILK**
½ CUP RAW CASHEWS	**¾ CUP SUGAR**
½ CUP PLUS 2 TABLESPOONS RAISINS	**¼ TEASPOON GROUND CARDAMOM**
1 CUP DURUM WHEAT SEMOLINA FLOUR	**¼ TEASPOON SAFFRON THREADS**

1. Heat 1 tablespoon of the butter in a medium nonstick sauté pan over medium-low heat. Add the cashews and cook, stirring, until golden, about 2 minutes. Remove and set aside on paper towels. Add the raisins and cook, stirring, until they puff up and become dark golden, about 1 minute. Remove and set aside on paper towels.

2. Put the pan over medium heat. When hot, add the semolina flour and cook, stirring, until it is slightly darkened, has a fragrant roasted scent, and is coarser in texture, about 6 minutes. Transfer to a bowl and set aside.

3. Rinse the flour from the pan and return it to medium heat. Add 1½ cups water and the milk and bring just to a boil. Add the sugar, cardamom, and saffron. Simmer until the sugar dissolves, about 3 minutes.

4. Reduce the heat to low and add the semolina flour a little at a time, alternating with the raisins and cashews, stirring well, until the mixture thickens, after 5 to 6 minutes. Add the remaining 4 tablespoons butter and mix thoroughly until combined.

5. Remove from the heat. Pour the mixture into a 12 x 9-inch ungreased baking pan and smooth the surface with the back of a spoon. Cover with plastic wrap pressed against the surface and set aside to cool. Cut into diamonds or squares and serve at room temperature.

Monsoon Rice Pudding

Monsoon Rice Pudding Sweet but not cloying, this rice pudding carries hints of vanilla and richness from the raisins. You can make this several hours before serving. I like to serve this pudding in little ramekins after a light dinner. In the summer it is delicious served chilled, and in the winter, it is comforting eaten warm. SERVES 6

½ CUP WHITE BASMATI RICE	4½ TABLESPOONS SUGAR
5 CUPS WHOLE MILK	1 TABLESPOON UNSALTED BUTTER
1 VANILLA BEAN	¼ CUP RAISINS

1. Wash the rice by gently rubbing the grains with your fingers in a bowl of water. When the water becomes cloudy, drain the water and repeat the process until the water is clear. Drain the rice.

2. Bring the milk and rice to a boil in a large heavy saucepan over medium-high heat. Reduce the heat to low and cook, stirring every so often, for 10 minutes.

3. Split the vanilla bean lengthwise and scrape the seeds into the pot. Add the vanilla bean as well. Continue cooking, stirring every so often, for 35 minutes, or until the pudding has a thick, creamy consistency and the rice is tender. Add the sugar, reduce the heat to low, and cook for 5 minutes.

4. Meanwhile, heat the butter in a small skillet over medium-low heat. Add the raisins and cook until they puff up, about 1 minute. Add to the pudding and mix well to combine. Reduce the heat to low and cook for 3 minutes. Remove from the heat. Serve warm or chilled.

Pumpkin Coconut Pudding
Known in Bali as *kue labu*, or pumpkin cake, this is a darling recipe that I would whip up during my cooking days at the Four Seasons in Bali. This delicate pudding can be made with either pumpkin or corn, especially in the late summer and early autumn, when they are both in season. I love both variations for their delicate texture and creamy flavor. The more finely you grate the pumpkin, the lighter and silkier the taste will be. Just before serving, top the pudding with freshly whipped cream and a sprig of fresh mint for a lovely presentation. SERVES 6

ONE 1-POUND PUMPKIN OR BUTTERNUT SQUASH, PEELED, SEEDED, AND GRATED (ABOUT 1¼ CUPS)

1⅔ CUPS CANNED COCONUT MILK (PAGE 26)

½ CUP SUGAR

½ TEASPOON SALT

ONE 12-INCH FRESH PANDAN LEAF OR 1 VANILLA BEAN, SPLIT

⅓ CUP PLUS 2 TABLESPOONS CORNSTARCH MIXED WITH ½ CUP WATER

1. Set up a steamer by bringing a couple of inches of water to a boil in a large pot. Place the pumpkin in the steamer insert and set the insert over the boiling water. Cover and steam for 5 minutes over medium heat. Remove from the heat and set aside.

2. Combine the coconut milk, sugar, salt, and pandan leaf in a medium saucepan over medium heat and bring just to a boil.

3. Slowly whisk the cornstarch mixture into the coconut milk. When the mixture starts to thicken, add the steamed pumpkin, stirring constantly until you have a smooth batter. Remove from the heat and pour into six 6-ounce ramekins. Allow to cool completely in the refrigerator. Serve chilled.

Resources

Apna Bazar
2245 148th Avenue NE
Bellevue, WA 98007
425-644-6887
apnabazarusa.com

Whole dried spices, pure chile powder, korma powder, turmeric, curry leaves

Grocery Thai
Los Angeles, CA
818-469-9407
grocerythai.com

Golden Boy fish sauce, tamarind, fresh aromatics, roasted chile paste, canned coconut milk and cream, dried rice noodles

Kalustyan's
123 Lexington Avenue
New York, NY 10016
212-683-3451
kalustyans.com

Whole dried spices and ground spices, curry leaves

99 Ranch Market
18230 East Valley Highway
Kent, WA 98032
425-251-9099
99ranch.com

Canned coconut milk and cream, kaffir lime leaves, lemongrass, Thai basil, bird's-eye chiles, galangal, tamarind, curry leaves, oyster sauce, fish sauce, shrimp paste, spices, dried shrimp, great selection of fresh noodles and tofus, kecap manis

Penzeys Spices
Multiple locations
800-741-7787
penzeys.com

Whole dried spices and ground spices

The Spice House
1031 North Old World Third Street
Milwaukee, WI 53203
888-488-0977

1512 North Wells Street
Chicago, IL 60610
312-274-0378
thespicehouse.com

Whole dried spices and ground spices

Temple of Thai

22663 Quail Avenue
Carroll, IA 51401
877-811-8773
templeofthai.com

Fish sauce, roasted chile paste, oyster
sauce, palm sugar, rice powder

Uwajimaya

519 Sixth Avenue South
Seattle, WA 98104
206-624-6248
uwajimaya.com

Excellent seafood, selection of soy
sauces, Asian greens, tofu, noodles,
ginger, Sriracha sauce

Viet Wah

6040 Martin Luther King Jr. Way
Seattle, WA 98118
206-760-8895

1320 South Jackson Street
Seattle, WA 98104
206-329-1399
vietwah.com

Pandan leaves, Thai basil, kaffir lime
leaves, lemongrass, curry leaves,
tamarind, shrimp paste, kecap manis,
fish sauce, huge selection of chiles,
coconut milk and cream, potato
starch, palm sugar, candlenuts, shrimp
paste and a complete range of Southeast
Asian ingredients

Acknowledgments

This book is the result of the love, joy, and support from many dear friends. My heartfelt thanks go out to them:

Joy Tutela, a determined, compassionate agent and lovely friend, who nurtured my proposal with unflagging support from the beginning, and David Black, for believing in the project and me.

Rica Allannic, my talented editor, who cared for this book with her meticulous attention to the text and hard work; her assistant, Kathleen Fleury; Marysarah Quinn, creative director and designer extraordinaire, for her beautiful, artistic touch on every page. Thank you for making this book so outstanding. Christine Tanigawa, production editor, and Joan Denman, production manager, for devoting their professional time and holding the project together. My publicist, Ava Kavyani, for helping to make this book a success.

My mentor, Mufleh, a precious friend and pillar of strength without whom this book would not have been possible. You inspire me. I am ever so grateful to you for this. Dinarshad & Associates, for taking beautiful and memorable photographs during our travels in Malaysia. Din, thank you for your devotion to this project.

Charles, my cousin-brother, who painstakingly and passionately pieced together details about our family history. In Malaysia, Mr. Siva Valentine, for his valuable guidance.

My dedicated friends and treasured cooking students Anita Coke, Maureen and Jennifer Haim, Rosemarie Howard, Ruth Hunter, Lawrence Kurfiss, Heather MacMaster, Charles Miller, Hee-Won Patten, Jan Place, and Belinda Pollard, for testing recipes, their support, and appreciating my cooking in every class for the last ten years. I am also grateful to the many additional students who eagerly tested my recipes.

My immediate family, my sons Anton and Zachary, my sunshine and my joy. Thank you for your patience and understanding and for loving my cooking. Basil, Kate, and Uncle Karu for all your support. And most of all, I give God the glory for making this book possible.

Index

Page numbers in *italics* indicate photographs.

About the Author

Christina Arokiasamy, of Indian descent,
was raised in Kuala Lumpur, Malaysia.
She has a degree in public relations. She
began her culinary career working in
her family's kitchen and spice stall before
cooking in various Four Seasons resorts
throughout Southeast Asia. Christina opened
the Spice Merchant's Cooking School in the
Pacific Northwest where she lives with her
family. She also organizes and leads cultural
and culinary tours to Southeast Asian
destinations.